T0115087

Finding Peace in Chaos

E3: EMOTIONAL ENERGETIC EVOLUTION, MUSCLE TESTING AND PERSONALITY

Dr. William D. Mehring

BALBOA.
PRESS

A DIVISION OF HAY HOUSE

ISBN: 978-1-4525-5090-9 (sc)
ISBN: 978-1-4525-5091-6 (e)

Library of Congress Control Number: 2012908046

Balboa Press books may be ordered through booksellers or by contacting:

Balboa Press
A Division of Hay House
1663 Liberty Drive
Bloomington, IN 47403
www.balboapress.com
1-(877) 407-4847

Contents

Dedication

I dedicate this book to fatherhood and to my son. My father died when I was seven months old and I spent much of my life healing from that loss. I was given the greatest gift when my amazing son was born. Watching his joy and playing with him, I was able to father him like I wish I had been fathered. The gift of fatherhood is to experience loving and being loved unconditionally. It is a gift I wish I could have given to my father, and he to his father, who also died when he was young.

I wrote this book to help people heal themselves and others, so that everyone can live their highest and best lives. However, upon reflection, my true motivation for this work is I wanted my son to know me better. I want my life's work to help him find peace in his life. My wish is that every time he reads this book, he will know me and himself even more.

Forward

I COME TO WILLIAM MEHRING'S work as a client. He was highly recommended by another healing professional who had taken the E3: Emotional Energetic Evolution training and demonstrated it for me. As a therapist, I am always eager to know about innovative methods; especially those that reach down to powerful unconscious belief systems that shape our behavior and choices. This initial demonstration of the E3 method uncovered a deep connection between feelings of being burdened financially at the time, and my father's burdened state of mind when I was born. What was revealed resonated as true and, without any great effort, I was pleased that a whole series of positive decisions and actions resulted from what I learned in that session. That healing is still unfolding in my life and has led to a reduction of financial stress and other responsibilities that were not serving me.

I decided to see Dr. Mehring personally and embarked on a short series of sessions. These sessions deepened my awareness and catalyzed the forward movement that had been sparked in the demonstration by our mutual friend. A long-time proponent of muscle testing, I was very pleased to see that he uses applied kinesiology to find the truth in the body. I learned early on in my career as a therapist, and as a client of many body-mind modalities, that the body never lies. If you learn nothing else from this book, then you will have received a great deal. However, there is more.

As all therapists know, what expresses externally in our lives is formed by what has been going on internally for a long time. Through his years of knowledge and experienced gained as a chiropractor, and still more years of psychological study and practice, Will has arrived at an elegant approach to finding and reframing outworn belief systems. Using the client's body as a guide to soul truth, Will bypasses the chattering left-brain, which so frequently overpowers talk therapy. To use a Hollywood term, he cuts to the chase.

As a specialist in applied creativity, I know well the power of the right brain. Will taps into the emotional reality of the right hemisphere as well as the intuitive guidance that flows through it. Ultimately, his method is balancing because he helps the client articulate in words their old beliefs and new choices. As a journal therapy innovator, I was very pleased to see that Will assigns journaling to his clients. He did not have to convince me that journal homework would deepen the process and lead me to the results that I desired.

Will also brings a finely tuned gift that is absolutely necessary for any good therapist: intuition. He knows how to open himself, listen to the client's truth and tap into the universal healing wisdom that is available to all of us. For that reason, he truly is a trustworthy guide on the path of emotional energetic evolution.

As an astute observer of human behavior, Will also uses a highly effective color-based personality system related to chakra work in his healing methods. This system sheds a lot of light not only on the client's own behavior, but also on the actions and motivations of other people. This has a profound effect on interactions with friends, loved ones, co-workers and the like. Acceptance of ourselves for who we are as well as others, is the key factor, as are the tools for conscious change that Will provides. I recommend this book to anyone who is seeking inner peace in a world of chaos.

Lucia Capacchione, Ph.D., art therapist and author of The Power of Your Other Hand and Recovery of Your Inner Child.

Introduction

MY PURPOSE IN WRITING THIS work is to share a process I've developed called E3: Emotional Energetic Evolution, and to guide you in applying these therapeutic techniques in your healing practice and in your own life. Ultimately, this book is about the importance of listening to the voice of the soul.

Twelve years after I began my chiropractic practice, I suffered a vestibular injury which altered my balance mechanism and left me with chronic exertion headaches. Suffering from pain and poor balance, it was impossible for me to continue my chiropractic work, which was my passion. I had to figure out another way to live a happy, productive life. My true learning began during the subsequent four years, which turned out to be the most disharmonious years I'd ever experienced.

I opened a boat dealership, a seasonal business requiring long hours and a frenzied pace. That business brought out my obsessive and competitive nature as I strived to outsell all the other boat dealers. If I lost a deal to another boat dealership, I would become very upset. Boat manufacturers reward dealers who have the highest sales regardless of their tactics or ethics, so even my moral compass was challenged in this environment. I became progressively more angry and my behavior more cutthroat. I pushed harder to close more deals and climb to financial success. As a competitive person, I was no stranger to the body's stress response but this new work environment was the epitome of stress combined with chaos. It brought out my issues of scarcity, of not being good enough and of not being valued. I could not find inner peace no matter how hard I tried.

Outwardly, everything looked great. I had received many awards and had the highest sales per capita. I also had one of the highest customer satisfaction ratings of all the dealerships for this national manufacturer. I was successful, confident and seemingly on top of the world. Unfortunately, all this was fueled by fear and I lived in a constant state of trying to prove to myself and to the world that I was good enough, acceptable, and lovable. I had very little time with my wife and baby, and lost most of my friends. Even worse, I was unable to see all of this happening. My fear-based striving was my attempt to fill up a black hole of endless hunger that could never be filled.

Everything backfired. Instead of fixing the problem that I was trying to escape, I created the very thing I feared: feeling not good enough. In my blindness to my dysfunctional belief system and addiction to wrong actions, I said and did things that created more chaos in my life. On some level, I knew that I had to change and transform my beliefs and actions in order to save my life.

One day, while I was working late, a message bubbled up from deep within me that said, "You are killing yourself" and I knew it was true. I went to work the next day and announced to everyone that I would be selling the business. This came as a shock to everyone, especially my business partner, with whom I had to resolve many differences. However, the phone soon rang with an offer to purchase the dealership.

I was unfamiliar with the concept of "manifesting your destiny" at that time, but I have come to realize that is exactly what happened. The boat dealership sold, my partner became an employee of the new owner and I was free but that freedom came with a weighty responsibility. I had to deal with my fears and was forced to resolve my issues of self-worth, scarcity, productivity, control, and acceptance. That process allowed me to restructure my beliefs, personal laws, and other significant elements in my life.

I knew I needed to heal myself but I was unable to completely let go of the obsession to be productive. I sought ways of being productive and competitive within the framework of my healing process and athletics was the answer. I had been a competitive water skier but was no longer able to water ski due to my vestibular injury. Instead, I began to physically work hard swimming and cycling and soon I was with a group of people training for triathlons. I enjoyed the community and the training, but I also began practicing Qi Gong. This traditional Taoist practice incorporates intention, meditation, relaxation, physical movement, mind-body integration, and breathing exercises. I practiced the healing technique, known as the Bone Cleanse. This technique moves the universal life force energy throughout the body, replacing the old stagnant energy, which no longer serves you, with vital neutral energy. I worked to bring my life's unhealthy patterns to the forefront of my awareness so that I could engage with and transform them. I knew at the deepest level that my very life depended upon this work, and I never questioned it. I had to be willing to embrace the changes that were set before me. I invited the universe to show me the way and worked on walking through each door with open arms.

As part of the triathlon training, I rode my bike deep into the backcountry, and then ran on a trail that braided along a river. Once I was deep under the canopy of the oaks and sycamore trees, I would sit and meditate on simply receiving. Receiving is the ability to take in all that is going on around without having any thoughts or judgment about it. You perceive it, and then it is gone. I cleared my mind, grounded myself in the sensations of living and listened to, smelled, and tasted the air. Purple, magenta and green colors appeared before my closed eyes. I began to feel a greater awareness of the infinite energetic field of which I was a part. As I experienced the complete absence of *doing*, the complete presence of receiving grew larger and larger. Much to my surprise, I began to see that many of the events and interactions of my life were unhealthy. Each time I envisioned something I needed to transform, I would seek out the people involved and I'd say to them, "I did something to you that I didn't like. My behavior was based on these underlying intentions and/ or fears. If I were to do it over, this is how I would behave today." Once I started this process, I was compelled to continue this spring cleaning for my soul. This important process changed my life on many levels.

This deep introspection became a habit for me and it was a habit that became self-perpetuating because it led to harmonization and healing. I believe that healing one's deep wounds is the sweetest nectar of life. I believe you can heal or harmonize any situation that has occurred in your life at any time and the healing result will be the same whether you work on it immediately after the situation occurs or years later. It's never too late but we must be mindful of the tendency to procrastinate. We come up with logical if not honorable reasons not to embrace our fears. We tend to look for excuses for our behaviors and actions. But this procrastination can steal away the life you long for. I think of people on their deathbed who feel compelled to tell their family and friends about the things they would have done differently or things they wished they had said. Sometimes it takes the death process to see that the most important thing in life is to express our inner truth and affection and not run away from our fears.

Six months into my process of self introspection and healing, my wife convinced me to see a dermatologist to evaluate a freckle on my chest that had grown dramatically over the last year and a half. The dermatologist recommended removal and biopsy. After the procedure, he called with the results, indicating there was good news and bad news. I asked if I could hear the bad news first hoping to end the conversation on an upbeat note. The doctor told me the bad news was that the biopsy confirmed malignant melanoma but the good news was that the disease looked as if it was going through a rare spontaneous remission, uncommon for this type of skin cancer. The dermatologist also said there were no signs of malignant tentacles spreading from the skin cancer and that the freckle might have fallen off on its own in a couple of months. I knew malignant melanoma had less than a 5% five year survival rate but the pathology report indicated the remission process had begun about six months earlier. The doctor asked, "What have you been doing differently recently?" I told him about the emotional work I began six months earlier and he recommended I keep it up.

I followed this advice and ultimately realized I had to return to my "soul print" as a healer. Since I could no longer be a chiropractor, I returned to graduate school for my Master's degree in psychology and philosophy, as well as training in homeopathy and hypnotherapy. I took classes in comparative religion. Ultimately, I realized I was hiding in school and that it was time to begin helping others. Even more important, it was time to openly use my intuition and my kinesthetic appreciation of energy in my healing work.

This inspired me to develop E3: Emotional Energetic Evolution, the basis for this book. I wanted to create a technique that represented my journey of self discovery, searching to find my place in the healthcare realm after my injury. I wanted E3 to be accessible to all those seeking to help others all the while developing a sense of connection to their own inner wisdom and healing potential.

E3 can be used on oneself, or to facilitate healing work in others. It is designed to find peace in chaos and to cultivate the ability to hear and trust inner wisdom. E3 is useful for parents, children, students, really anyone seeking to connect to their inner wisdom when making life decisions. It is also useful for psychologists, social workers, chiropractors, medical doctors and healing professionals from all disciplines.

Although E3 incorporates principles of psychotherapy, homeopathy, hypnotherapy and philosophy, it is at its core a progression and diversification of applied kinesiology. Applied kinesiology was pioneered in 1964 by American chiropractor, Dr. George Goodheart Jr. He showed that the practitioner could have an ongoing conversation with a consciousness that resides within the patient's body. The chiropractic term for this is the innate, but psychologists might refer to this as the subconscious mind or the higher self. Philosophers would term this the soul. I have often imagined Dr. Goodheart puzzling over how to communicate with the wisdom of the inner workings of the body. It is hard to ascertain with certainty about these communication pathways yet this brings valuable information about the emotional issues that bring about disease and protracted stress within the body, as well as solutions to remedy dysfunction in the body.

Dr. Goodheart wanted to find a way for the body to speak to him, a way to access the body's inner consciousness and knowledge without the conscious mind hijacking the conversation. He was looking for a bodily system that would show changes quickly without any detrimental effects. He found that the muscular system was ideal because muscles can manifest changes in strength rapidly and then exhibit gradations of strength in response to stimuli and other input. Dr. Goodheart began to use the comparative strength function of muscles to help guide him in treating his patients. For a very long time, muscle testing and applied kinesiology were used exclusively by chiropractors. Because of its efficacy, muscle testing is now used to guide physicians and healers in every discipline. Muscle testing is similar to a lie detector test in that it affirms or negates answers to questions based on whether a muscle tests strong or weak.

I believe many chiropractic physicians, especially the old-timers, developed their diagnostic sense based on feelings, not logic. I wonder how many of those doctors were using their intuitive skills but never told anyone. The more I listened to intuitive information and figured out how to translate it, the finer tuned and more reliable my own intuition became and the more I listened.

The hardest part for me was moving this intuitive knowledge from the realm of a party trick to a functional diagnostic and treatment modality that could be put into practice. Once I realized that my patients were interested in healing above anything else, I put aside my fears about using intuition in diagnostics and began to employ this technique in my work. This shift was largely responsible for my success in facilitating the healing process. It was challenging to be different from the norm and some people were frightened or skeptical of this work, but many welcomed it. I also began to find other practitioners speaking my language and pursued formal training in energy work with two different Qi Gong masters, Ken Cohen and Hong Liu; and one Shao Lin priest, Yun Xiang Tseng.

Our internal beliefs carry within them a code of conduct about how we should act as well as how others should act. These rules and our actions have been carefully constructed and fortified by thousands if not millions of experiences, experiences which have filtered through our psychobiological make up. During our life, we have created an immense matrix of, "if this, then that." This creates a conditioned response for most situations that come up in life. The matrix will use its best guess as a response each time we come upon a new condition but this leads to many dysfunctional errors. The mind has to as close to a previous experience as possible to figure out what to do. Early on, when we haven't figured out how to contend with a situation, we sort through the matrix and find a response that is only remotely similar to the situation at hand. So the response you come up with can be very wrong for the situation and this is one way in which you can create a path with pitfalls or negative repercussions.

Let me give you a simplified example that still carries truth. Imagine a young child who wants attention and realizes that he gets it when he cries. As the child grows older, and wants attention or wants a new toy, what do you think his strategy will be? The parallel is that most of our actions and defense mechanisms are based on the realities and experiences of our very young selves. As we mature, we outgrow or evolve some of those belief systems and their resulting actions, but sometimes this can only be achieved through sustained practice, determination, and self-knowledge. The E3 process can guide you along this path.

While there are many possible healthcare applications for E3, anyone who wants to find peace amidst the chaos of everyday life can train themselves to use it effectively. The E3 technique teaches you to communicate with your inner self or soul on a regular basis to find out what is causing stress. It then provides a path to transform this stress into peace and the result is a better life. I use the E3 technique to help me navigate every day. For example, my son has trouble with his ankles and knees, exacerbated when wearing certain shoes. So I screen shoes through muscle testing. He has no pain when he wears shoes that tested as clear. Muscle testing and the E3 technique can discover food allergies or sensitivities or the presence of harmful chemicals. The applications for tapping into your inner wisdom in the home and through life are endless. We question our decisions all day long wondering which choice will serve us the best. If the answer is not immediately clear, muscle testing can help to ascertain the answer.

Healthcare providers can use the E3 technique in a variety of ways. Massage therapists can use E3 to pinpoint dysfunction and focus their treatment. The body's wisdom can be harnessed to assess musculoskeletal dysfunction. The E3 process determines which muscles should be stretched and which should be strengthened. Acupuncturists can quickly screen through the various channels or meridians to accurately assess which points to use in treatment and which ones are unnecessary. The outcome is an improved treatment success rate with their patients. Nutritionists and homeopaths can use E3 to determine treatment regimens. Dosages, dilutions, how many times a day and which meals need added supplementation can all be tested using muscle testing. So as you can see, the applications for muscle testing in the healing arts are vast. I look forward to the day when medical doctors use muscle testing to help confirm diagnoses and affirm treatment. Imagine testing which drug has the least side effects for each individual patient, or testing to find new substances that can mitigate the toxic effects of some prescription medications.

Many people, including myself, started with simple applications before branching into more complex situations. It is a tool that pierces through time, compensatory mechanisms, and misinformation in the conscious mind, to help aid in healing. It can help us in situations where we lack diagnostic technology. Most important, it can help unwind our emotional turmoil. The more you use muscle testing, the more accurate you will become. The more accurate you become, the more you will trust your own feelings and intuition. Using the muscle testing of applied kinesiology allows you to access the elegant and sentient wisdom that is within you and assists you with the big decisions of your life.

I will add a caveat here. I have been asked if this technique can be used in commerce or business dealings. Muscle testing becomes unreliable when used to determine advantage or increased profitability. Healthcare practitioners intend their work for the good of the patient not personal or monetary gain. E3 works to connect to our inner wisdom, our higher consciousness. I have confirmed what others have found, that this technique will only work to promote a higher good not to choose winning lottery numbers. However, if your business's mission statement is to help others while helping yourself, this technique is for you. It can help you make decisions in business that will benefit you, your employees and your customers all at the same time.

Part I of this book is an introduction to the E3 process and philosophy, how we create belief systems and actions, and how we can reconstruct them. It also includes the four basic personality colors. Part II teaches how to use muscle testing and the E3 process for personal or client healing work. If you want simple answers regarding nutrition, allergens or decisions relating to your highest good, or if you want to facilitate healing for others, all of the information is contained in this section. Part III takes a final look at what a life guided by the higher self rather than the ego looks like. It engages you in the transformation process and encourages you to stay on the path of finding peace in chaos. I invite you to use E3 and hope it opens many doors for you and helps in healing those with whom you work.

PART I

Chapter 1

DEEP HEALING AND THE E3 PROCESS

I WAS SITTING IN A dark psychology classroom, rays of light shining over my shoulder onto a silver screen. The loud rhythmic clicking of the projector distracted me from the chatter of the other students. The film was introducing case histories of various personality disorders. This seemingly inconsequential film had me riveted. I was particularly interested in the case of a woman with multiple personality disorder, and the manifestation of her two very distinct personalities. I was fascinated that whenever she shifted from one personality to the other, her physical appearance changed dramatically as well. There were demonstrative morphological changes in her posture, facial expressions, and gait. What wasn't clear to me then but is very clear now, is that these physical changes were in response to changes in her thoughts, beliefs and interactions with life events. Her two personalities had completely different personal beliefs therefore she reacted differently to the same life events depending on which personality was present.

This phenomenon is much the same in the case of monozygotic twins. These are twins that occur when a single egg is fertilized to form one zygote, which then divides into two separate embryos. The twins have identical DNA, but likely do not share the same personalities. Two genetically identical beings should develop into virtually identical adults but they do not. This proves that personality is not rigidly tied to DNA. Also, these genetically identical twins do not necessarily develop the same propensity for disease, longevity, and IQ. Each twin not only has a unique hardwired personality but each experiences life in their own unique way. From the very moment of conception, each twin's unique personality steers their destiny and their physical development. As the twins age, they become more distinct.

Traditional psychological theory further supports the idea that personality is linked to physicality. The psychologist William Herbert Sheldon Jr. correlated body morphology to personality type, organizing people into three primary types: endomorph, ectomorph and mesomorph. There are other theories as well correlating body shape, posture, and facial expressions with personalities and disease, particularly in the field of bioenergetics. The idea that personality can alter the physicality of the human being as it grows and develops has become clear to me as a physician. The longer we live the more our thoughts manifest our physicality.

The multiple personality patient in the film had different physical pathology in each of her personalities. One personality had symptoms of systemic lupus erythematosus (SLE). The symptoms of this autoimmune disease are a red or malar rash below her eyes, inflamed and painful joints, and a mildly elevated blood level of rheumatoid factor. When the patient manifested the second personality for a sustained period of time, those SLE symptoms would disappear. The second personality had cardiac symptoms, including mitral valve pathology. It became clear to me that dis-ease was impermanent and that it could be changed and even eradicated by altering the personality. Idiopathic diseases came to my mind. These diseases have no known cause or origin and they often have an autoimmune component, where the body shuts down or even attacks itself for no known reason.

Here is an example from my own practice. I received a call from a distressed mother whose son had gone off to college and he started to experiment with drugs. While under the influence of the drugs, her son was involved in an altercation and sustained a head trauma. His behavior became more extreme, to the point he would be classified as psychotic. Though the head trauma caused no physical damage, he outwardly looked so different that his family and friends had a hard time believing he was the same guy. His mother, his girlfriend and many of his long-term friends were baffled because his whole demeanor changed completely and the more paranoid and delusional he became, the more pronounced the change was in his physical appearance. Unfortunately, these psycho-emotional changes also affected his internal physiology which in turn affected his overall health status. Physicality is intimately connected to the energetic blueprint of the body.

The E3 technique starts with energetics. This term comes from the physics principle that all things of this world exist in a minimum of two different states. One state is physical and the other is energetic and scientists have come to realize that matter exists in both these states simultaneously. Everything in our physical world is made up of atomic and eventually, subatomic particles. Albert Einstein devoted over twenty years of his life discerning whether subatomic particles were particles of physicality, or if they existed as waveforms of energy. Today we know matter exists in both states and even more exciting is the ease with which matter can move from one form to another.

This is important in E3 because the laws of physics remind us that consciousness, thoughts, and beliefs are all energetic forms, dwelling in the energetic realm. Energy is the precursor to physicality, so our thoughts are the precursor to our physical body. Science is increasingly supporting the hypothesis that the thoughts we carry within our minds create the physicality of our bodies. That physicality can be one of harmony and health, but it can also be one of chaos and dis-ease. This tells us that harmonizing things on an energetic level has great potential for altering our physical bodies. It is important that our energetic blueprint is free of stressors that can lead to the deterioration of the physical body.

Energetics can be used as a guide both diagnostically and as a treatment modality. When a patient comes for treatment without knowing the specific issue causing their stress, I let the energetic patterns of the body guide the treatment. I run my hand over the central part of the body without physically touching the patient, but sensing and screening for areas that lack energy flow. Kinesthetically, this feels like a decreased or absence of tingling in my hands and indicates to me that there is dysfunction in those areas. I verify my findings with a muscle test. After I identify the problem area, E3 is the vehicle to access the subconscious to receive diagnostic information. There are many diagnostic tests that can also be used as well for definitive diagnoses if physical dis-ease is found.

Energetics can also be used as a healing modality. The consciousness has the capacity to move, focus and intend changes through energetics. It is an imperative part of a healing practice to teach people how to treat themselves with the infinite life force of the universe. This is evidenced by the growing mountain of research regarding the power of prayer and energy in the healing process. Daniel J. Benor M.D., author of <u>Spiritual Healing: Scientific Validation of a Healing Revolution</u>, has created volumes of research with scientific methodology proving the efficacy of energy healing.

The first step in the E3 technique is to gain access to the issues that need to be resolved. The problem areas are localized through muscle testing. I begin by concentrating on the painful or dysfunctional area but I also utilize the chakras that correspond to a problem area. A chakra is a processing center for the body's energy, including emotional energy, conscious thoughts, and thoughts of every cell in the body. I use a seven chakra system, referenced on the following Emotional Chakra and Ethereal Chakra charts.

Chakras and Their Emotions

Brain (General) B
Pineal (Posterior) P
Pituitary P
Testability pt T
Brain laterality or block
Governing Vessel pt GV
Collecting Vessel pt CV

Additional CV/GV point
Organ, skin
tip points or skin contact

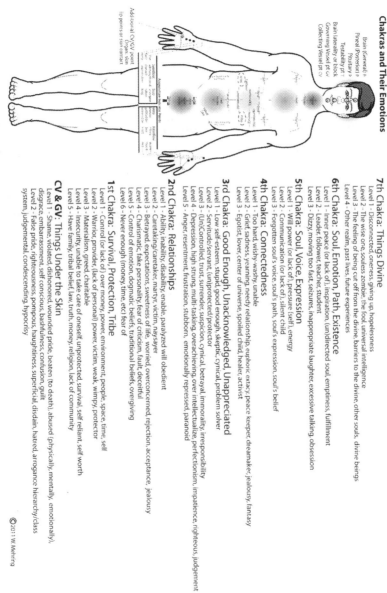

7th Chakra: Things Divine
Level 1 - Disconnected, oneness, giving up, hopelessness
Level 2 - The wise one, souless zombie, the fool, universal intelligence
Level 3 - The feeling of being cut off from the divine, barriers to the divine, other souls, divine beings
Level 4 - Other realm, past lives, future experiences

6th Chakra: Soul, Emotion, Path, Existence
Level 1 - Inner peace (or lack of), inspiration, (un)directed soul, emptiness, fulfillment
Level 2 - Leader, follower, teacher, student
Level 3 - Dizzy, moving too fast, seizures, inappropriate laughter, excessive talking, obsession

5th Chakra: Soul, Voice, Expression
Level 1 - Will power (or lack of), pressure (self), energy
Level 2 - Communication (or lack of), silent child
Level 3 - Forgotten soul's voice, soul's path, soul's expression, soul's belief

4th Chakra: Connectedness
Level 1 - Too hard, wishy-washy, unable
Level 2 - Grief, sadness, yearning, needy relationship, euphoric extacy, peace keeper, dreamaker, jealousy, fantasy
Level 3 - Egotist, lover, center of universe, spoiled child, healer, activist

3rd Chakra: Good Enough, Unacknowledged, Unappreciated
Level 1 - Low self-esteem, stupid, good enough, skeptic, cynical, problem solver
Level 2 - Servitude/servant, (un)protected/protector
Level 3 - (Un)Controlled, trust, surrender, suspicion, cynical, betrayal, immorality, irresponsibility
Level 4 - Charismatic, fake personality, fear of criticism, fault, deceitful
Level 5 - Depression, high strung, multi-tasking, overachieving, over intellectualize, perfectionism, impatience, righteous, judgement
Level 6 - Anger, resentment, frustration, stubborn, emotionally repressed, paranoid

2nd Chakra: Relationships
Level 1 - Ability, inability, disability, enable, paralyzed will, obedient
Level 2 - Caretaking/caretaker, martyr, victim, naysayer
Level 3 - Betrayed, expectations, sweetness of life, worried, overconcerned, rejection, acceptance, jealousy
Level 4 - Insecurity, unable to take care of oneself, unprotected, survival, self reliant, self worth
Level 5 - Have family, tribal belief, law, truth, money, religion, lack of community
Level 6 - Control of emotion, dogmatic beliefs, traditional beliefs, overgiving
Level - Never enough (money, time, etc) fear of

1st Chakra: Survival, Protection, Tribe
Level 1 - Control (or lack of) over money, power, environment, people, space, time, self
Level 2 - Warrior, provider, (lack of personal) power, victim, weak, wimpy, protector
Level 3 - Materialism, greed, charitable

CV & GV: Things Under the Skin
Level 1 - Shame, violated, dishonored, wounded pride, beaten (to death), abused (physically, mentally, emotionally), disgrace, embarrassment, self conscious, bashfulness, confusion, guilt
Level 2 - False pride, righteousness, pompous, haughtiness, superficial, disdain, hatred, arrogance, hierarchy/class system, judgemental, condescending, hypocrisy

Diagram 1a. Emotional Chakras

Ethereal Chakra 8~15 / Physical Body Chakra 1~7

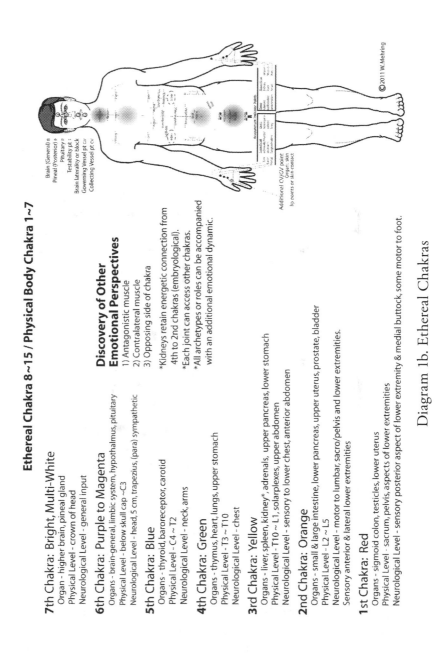

7th Chakra: Bright, Multi-White
Organ - higher brain, pineal gland
Physical Level - crown of head
Neurological Level - general input

6th Chakra: Purple to Magenta
Organs - brain-general, limbic system, hypothalmus, pituitary
Physical Level - below skull cap ~C3
Neurological Level - head, 5 cm, trapezius, (para) sympathetic

5th Chakra: Blue
Organs - thyroid, baroreceptor, carotid
Physical Level - C4 ~ T2
Neurological Level - neck, arms

4th Chakra: Green
Organs - thymus, heart, lungs, upper stomach
Physical Level - T3 ~ T10
Neurological Level - chest

3rd Chakra: Yellow
Organs - liver, spleen, kidney*, adrenals, upper pancreas, lower stomach
Physical Level - T10 ~ L1, solarplexes, upper abdomen
Neurological Level - sensory to lower chest, anterior abdomen

2nd Chakra: Orange
Organs - small & large intestine, lower pancreas, upper uterus, prostate, bladder
Physical Level - L2 ~ L5
Neurological Level - motor to lumbar, sacro/pelvis and lower extremities.
Sensory anterior & lateral lower extremities

1st Chakra: Red
Organs - sigmoid colon, testicles, lower uterus
Physical Level - sacrum, pelvis, aspects of lower extremities
Neurological Level - sensory posterior aspect of lower extremity & medial buttock, some motor to foot.

Discovery of Other Emotional Perspectives
1) Antagonistic muscle
2) Contralateral muscle
3) Opposing side of chakra

*Kidneys retain energetic connection from 4th to 2nd chakras (embryological).

*Each joint can access other chakras.

*All archetypes or roles can be accompanied with an additional emotional dynamic.

Additional CV/GV point:
lip points or skin contact

©2011 W.Mehring

Diagram 1b. Ethereal Chakras

To find the problem area, I test the strength of a strong muscle, usually in the arm or shoulder muscles. If the muscle goes weak while the painful area is touched or while you hold your hand over the associated chakra area, this indicates the area being screened is an area of dysfunction. This dysfunction can be emotional, physical, nutritional deficit, or something else.

Imagine a client who presents with a diagnosis of nervous stomach or stomach ulcers. The first thing I do is to touch the area right over the stomach, or the chakra that corresponds to that area. Then I test to see if the arm muscle goes weak. If it does, it identifies a problem. This is called therapy localization. I then must discern whether the problem is entirely physical or if there is an emotional component. I stop touching the area of the stomach and state, "Test the idea of a physical issue." I test the muscle strength again and if the muscle still goes weak, this determines that the problem is physical in nature. If the muscle remains strong, it indicates that the problem is not physical, and I would then evaluate if an emotional component is involved. It is important to always investigate the physical problem first. Problems in the physical realm take priority and may need immediate attention. The emotional problem often does not surface until you have revealed the physical problem.

So assuming I am dealing with a physical problem, I must differentiate and rule out the origins of the physical problem. I test possibilities such as bacterial infections, inadequate nutrition, allergies or something else. After I determine the origins of the physical problem, I test for what treatment or therapy will benefit or resolve it. I may test the efficacy of homeopathy, acupuncture, medication, chiropractic manipulative therapy, nutrition and even if further diagnostic evaluation is necessary. The muscle will go weak when I find the appropriate therapy.

My clinical experience has shown that dysfunction and dis-ease are common amongst patients who internalize stress. I define 'stress' as the result of beliefs or desires about events or people that conflict with one's expectations about how the world or people should be. I call the many stresses in our life 'emotional dynamics.' Some examples are loneliness, betrayal, disappointment, lack of control, or not feeling good enough.

Behind each of these emotional dynamics is a belief system that is in conflict with reality and is causing the person stress. The more we hold onto such beliefs, the more stress we have. The more stress we have, the more our body becomes handicapped and dis-eased. I believe that idiopathic and perhaps other dis-eases are a result of long-term emotional and energetic dysfunction. Further, certain personalities may be more prone to certain dis-eases.

Usually there are multiple layers and interwoven connections to an emotional dynamic. Take the issue of abandonment. Loss and grief are of the same nature as they manifest with similar feelings. But issues of control or the need for power might be connected to abandonment, if the patient experiencing abandonment tries to exert control over the people in order to keep them from leaving. Feelings of powerlessness or lack of control are not exactly the same as abandonment and grief but they can all be connected. One may need to navigate through each of these emotional dynamics before the core issue of abandonment can be released. Although there are guidelines and protocols associated with E3, emotions are not governed by logical patterns. The process of harmonizing the emotions will take many twists and turns.

Of course, there are other causative factors for dis-ease such as chemical contamination, pathogens, carcinogens, and trauma. There can also be hereditary factors that contribute. The personality creates a matrix of belief systems that dictate how we interpret and internalize our life events. If we can change our personality, and all that entails, we can affect our susceptibility to the dis-ease process. My own clinical and life experience brings me to believe that our physical well being depends on our actions and how we interpret the events of life. To reverse the dis-ease process, we must determine what part of our belief system is causing stress.

Every cell in the body has a unique consciousness, the capacity to perceive and process, and to give feedback. Our organs are colonies of cells that share a common function. Eastern medicine has long recognized that certain organs are more apt to process certain emotions. Some people process issues in their stomach with resulting ulcers or gastric reflux. Others process their stress in their intestines and suffer irritable bowel syndrome or colitis. Processing issues in the heart can result in arrhythmias, tachycardia, and high blood pressure. Back pain, tendonitis or fibromyalgia is often caused by holding stress in the muscles and connective tissue. People that hold stress in the neurologic system can end up with migraines and other neurological symptoms. Another classic example is people that harbor resentment. The classic place to hold and process this stress is in the kidneys. Of course, different people with different personalities could process the same issues in different parts of the body. E3 has the flexibility to allow the practitioner to find where the emotional dynamic is being processed.

Whatever the case, if we choose not to work on the issues, the life force energetically holds its breath. If this is the case, then after a time, the physicality begins to break down and it will manifest as dis-ease. I do not contend that every malady known to the human body comes from stress, but I believe it is accurate to say that all dis-eases have a psychological component and some dis-eases are a direct result of the chaos or stress within our consciousness. The exciting part of this work is that there are many ways of detecting emotional issues. Using therapy localization, the patient will be asked to recall a concept, a feeling, memories, dreams, or images as the practitioner touches the area of concern. If the arm muscle tests weak, the practitioner has localized the problem or issue. There are a plethora of doors that lead to quickly and efficiently accessing the issues that create dis-ease.

Another component in the E3 process is determining whether or not it is in the client's highest and best interest to use the next E3 tool called future probabilities. The future is not set in stone but is the outcome of a wave of collapsing probabilities. Sometimes crucial pieces in the puzzle have not yet been decided upon. Imagine how easily we would change our thoughts and behaviors if we knew who and what was involved when the issue resurfaced. We have trained ourselves to have a knee-jerk or conditioned response to most events in life; future possibility planning reinforces new behaviors. I look for who or what will be the trigger for a future event. I will be discussing this in depth in subsequent chapters.

How exactly does stress and chaos show up in the body as physical dis-ease? When dis-ease comes from a psychological paralysis or addiction to a non-harmonious belief system, it usually comes after years of dysfunction and warning signs. These are meant to awaken you to the fact that you have a belief system that must be altered. The usual response to fears and lack of control is the immediate release of neurochemicals such as adrenaline and epinephrine. These are the classic chemicals, among others, used by the body for the fight or flight response. Our cardiovascular system jumps into action, speeds up, and pushes fuel and oxygen throughout the muscular system. There is a price to pay for mobilizing these energy stores. The body can handle the infrequent physical stress of being chased by a saber-toothed tiger or attack by an enemy. If this response is continuously over used, the body becomes vulnerable to deterioration and dis-ease. These neurochemicals are also released due to psycho-emotional stress and thus can be present all day long. We cannot run fast enough or escape this and there is no time for recharging and repair. Psycho emotional stress is not the only reason for this neurochemical response. In today's world, we use the fight or flight mechanism to be productive, to multitask and to do battle at work. Most of us have become addicted to this chemical response and feel we cannot get through life without being jacked-up. Our addiction to adrenal producing substances such as caffeine is evidence for this.

The simple explanation is that every cell in our body responds to neurochemicals, hormones and the communications of thoughts and feelings. When we shut down or function out of depression, anger, fear or hurt, the cells follow suit. Internalizing negative thoughts means that the cells are living in a dis-eased state and the organs, which are comprised of these cells, become dis-eased in the emotional processing. Over time, the body collapses under the weight of the unrelenting stress and dysfunction and pathology ensues.

Neuro-endocrinologists have shown that every cell of the body has the ability to receive neurochemicals and to be emotional. Through the science of nanotechnology, scientists have shown that each cell makes noise, representing its voice and the sound appears to change based on what the cell encounters. Further, cellular biologists discuss the field effect in which all the body's cells simultaneously know what the rest of the body is thinking or feeling even before neurochemicals can reach them. This instantaneous knowing indicates that there is an energetic transmission of communication between the cells of the body. Scientists have observed these phenomena but are currently unable to prove the exact mechanism of how this energetic communication is occurring. The more we realize how much of our world exists in the energetic dimensions, the less three-dimensional it will look. Earlier in our history we went from a two-dimensional flat world to the three-dimensional world of a sphere. The next jump will be even more magnificent.

Our neurological, cardiovascular and immune systems are the physiologic systems that listen and are affected the most by our emotional states. Dysfunctional beliefs systems show up as stress. A good deal of the psycho-emotional stress occurs when we are disappointed that the people and the world around us do not behave as expected. In other words, no one is obeying our belief systems or personal laws. E3 is used to explore these belief systems. The patient is asked to distill which of his or her past core beliefs, personal codes or judgments are in conflict with reality. An individual might wrestle with abandonment, loss, betrayal, guilt, shame, and control or the lack thereof, to name a few issues. These dynamics usually form themes in our lives and these themes become the lens through which we interpret our life events regardless of what happened. For example, imagine someone who has a strong issue about abandonment and loss. Most of us realize that some relationships last longer than others but that ultimately, circumstances and relationships change and people may not be as close or available as they once were. A person without abandonment issues accepts this as the normal ebb and flow of life and may even view these changes as opportunities for new exciting relationships to be born. However, the person who is wrestling with this issue interprets each relationship change as catastrophic. They do not want anyone to leave them and appear clingy. The longer this emotional dynamic remains unresolved, the more powerful and consuming the abandonment and loss. I worked with one client whose abandonment issues had escalated to the point where she even mourned deeply the loss of the spiders that disappeared from the ceiling of her house. We must remember that the longer we avoid working with our fears and our emotional issues, the more prevalent they are.

A heightened sense of self awareness is very important in this process. It is difficult to see our own issues and dysfunctional behaviors because they have occurred over time and thus feel normal. I ask patients to carry around a small notepad to journal every time their particular emotional dynamic pops up. I make sure that the book is easy to carry but is just large enough to mildly irritate them so that they remember to use it. This is akin to tying a little bow around the finger. There are usually just a few entries to be found at their first follow-up visit with me, but the more they are aware and the more they do this work, the more they realize that nearly every action of their life is informed by fears and their larger issues.

When a person can say, "I realize that these emotional core issues are at play at least one hundred times a day. It's in everything I do," they have a good sense of self awareness. These people have done the work that holds the key to transformation when they start to feel repulsed by repeating the patterned behavior. They have the blueprint for change in their lives and can help others as well.

Once the dysfunctional theme or belief system is identified, the next step is to determine what event triggered this sensitization. This is a basic principle of psychological therapeutics: to access and transform the event that created the belief system in order to transform everything that follows. The idea is that if we find the first snowflake that started the avalanche, and catch it, we can stop the avalanche. It will be much harder to transform or change events or behaviors if this first or initial sensitizing event is not changed.

My mother's battle with colon cancer extended my understanding of the power of this work. She was diagnosed with Stage 3 colon cancer. This means that the dis-ease had spread throughout the tissue of the organ as well as into the lymph nodes. Both Stage 3 and Stage 4, indicate that the cancer is well developed and on the loose. Once the cancer cells have spread to the lymph nodes it is very likely that they will set up in other tissues in the body, which is known as metastatic cancer. She underwent surgery to resect one third of her lower intestine and chemotherapy was recommended as a follow-up.

When she was able, I took my mother to a healing place in the Rocky Mountains and we spent days investigating the emotional issues she was processing in her large intestine, and anywhere else issues were residing, using muscle testing. My mother had three interlocking issues of loss, grief and abandonment. When we accessed the initial sensitizing event, including when it occurred and who the players were in the situation, we began to unfold interactions that existed between her parents and her three siblings. The experiences she had perceived through her own eyes created the belief systems that coursed through every day of her life. The initial sensitizing event was not specific per se, but was a generalized feeling of not being loved by her mother from the age of two years old. This set up a life where she was prone to feeling abandoned by people around her and loss and grief were the linked emotions that amplified the abandonment. For days we worked out new ways of looking at the relationships in her life that were more harmonious and did not result in the feelings of abandonment. We also began meditation and Qi Gong healing, and evaluated nutritional, herbal, pharmaceutical or homeopathic substances that would help her healing process. This was not only a healing time for her individually but a wonderful time for the two of us. Many of the issues that stood between us were discussed, and we came to terms with each other in new ways.

My mother chose to use Chinese herbs, raw vegetable juicing, acupuncture, meditation, Qi Gong healing and continued emotional awakening for her therapy. Muscle testing indicated that these were the tools which were in her highest and best interest. She continued to consult with an oncologist but the little voice within her steered her away from chemotherapy. We went to her six-month post surgical checkup nervously but were calmed by the news that there was no sign of the cancer. At her five-year checkup, she remained cancer free.

Another example is a very dear friend of mine who was a massage therapist and asked me to consult on one of his patients with chronic pain. The patient was completely disabled, her spinal pain so intense that she could only stand for thirty minutes and sit for only five to ten minutes before she had to lie down. Using my hand as a way to sense the amount of Chi or life force that existed in different parts of her body, I screened for the area where I felt the least energy (This is a very easy way to access areas within someone's body that are processing stuck emotional issues. Developing a kinesthetic sense is not a mandate of the E3 technique; it just makes it a whole lot easier. The alternative is to use muscle testing to scan different areas or organs where emotions are being processed.). I felt the least energy movement in the first chakra. I then used muscle testing to determine the emotional dynamic that she was processing in this area, and found abandonment and fear of being alone were the core issues. Once I identified the emotional dynamic, I looked for the latest manifestation. She had lost her husband, a policeman who was shot and killed in the line of duty. Her low back pain began to develop shortly after his death. The pain was manageable until her son decided to become a policeman as well. The pain increased and spread up her spine shortly after her son suffered an injury in the line of duty. Luckily, he did not die but the pain grew worse when he returned to duty.

We had to find the first snowflake that put the issues in the forefront of her subconscious mind. The sensitizing event had occurred at the age of six, when she lost her father, also a police officer. She remembered her father leaving to go to work, and then later receiving the news that he had died in the line of duty. The story that she played repeatedly in her mind was that the important men in her life would die at work. This is why her pain did not get worse when her son was home recuperating, but it progressed when he returned to work. Each time he left, she feared that he would never come back. She was living in a constant state of fear, wondering if each day would be the day that she would get the phone call. Having this thought cycle through her mind was almost as powerful as having a loved one die every day. We had to reconstruct the initial sensitizing event and start by feeling it completely. So much of the healing comes from acknowledgment and awareness versus processing issues in darkness. The key to doing this work successfully is in creating harmonious new belief systems and actions.

I then asked the client to relax as I used mild hypnotherapy to reconstruct how she saw her life's events. The fact that her son not only became a police officer, but was also harmed in the line of duty, is one of those strange coincidences. It's as if the universe fed her the very situations she feared the most so that she could transcend them. About an hour and a half into this session she looked at me with utter astonishment. She told me that she had not sat this long in years. Even more astonishing was that she was not feeling low back pain. We continued to probe for any other layers or connections to other emotional issues. Soon we were done. We reviewed the issues to be aware of and I asked her to journal about all of her actions that were motivated by this fear of abandonment and being left alone. I planned to see her in a week for a follow-up.

She called three days later and told me her back was really sore. I asked her if she could connect the back pain to any thoughts or any incidences that may have sparked her fears but she told me it wasn't like that. She said this was good pain. She had been gardening the entire previous day and all of her muscles were very sore from her return to activity. Not every result is so dramatic; years of crippling spine pain which resolved in one treatment. She was yet another gift that demonstrated the incredible power of doing emotional work and I am grateful for the experience which affirmed my work was on track. My previous chiropractor training led me to believe I had to do something physical to achieve such change. After years of work in the emotional-energetic world, I will never under estimate its potential for change.

Our life experiences are consolidated and laid down in a pyramid formation, the organization of which is quite precise. The experiences are organized within the pyramid in accordance with associations and relationships. It is something like a three-dimensional crossword puzzle where associations are made vertically, horizontally, and diagonally in three-dimensional planes.

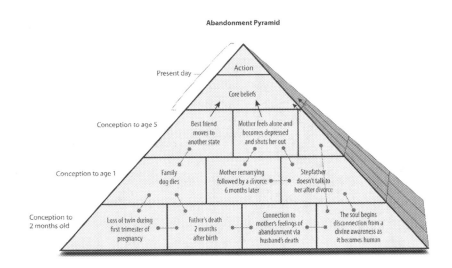

Diagram 2. The apex of the pyramid holds the actions that are the ultimate result of the beliefs generated from the person's life experience. The emotional dynamics that resonate the strongest will be determined by that personality. The person's personality will filter and transform all of life's events to be seen in a way that conforms to and activates their core issues.

When each of these pyramids is laid side-by-side with the apexes pointed towards the others in the center of the geodesic sphere, (Diagram 4) connections are made between one family of issues and another. This means that two issues may share the same experience.

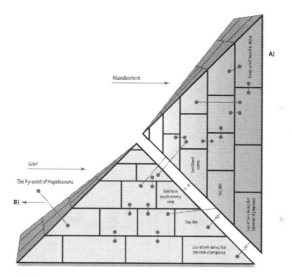

Diagram 3. Two Pyramids. Various pieces of the matrix will align if they share the same experience to an emotion in the same family of feelings. This creates the intricate connection of issue constellation.

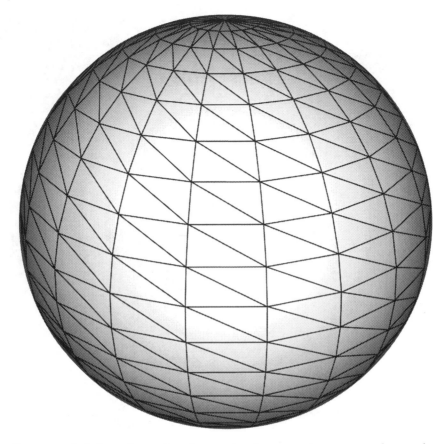

Diagram 4. Sphere. I imagine the matrix of our consciousness as a large sphere made up of many pyramids that catalog our interpretations of experiences: pyramids connecting the issue constellations formed in life. The outer layer has initial experiences. The deeper you go into the sphere, the more set in your ways of seeing life. The inner core is beliefs and actions that are held firmly by the interconnections and gravity of our consciousness. This model makes the outer crust the easiest to access and change. This is where E3 de-junks and reboots our matrix into how we wish it to be.

If there are several shared experiences harboring the same emotional issues, they will become linked. For example, judgment and the wish to control others can be coupled in the same circumstance. This would put the pyramid of judgment close to the issue of control. For each of us, the symbols of these global constellations are based on our makeup and our experiences.

Imagine being inside the matrix of the sphere where the boundaries between the different pyramids are lost. This is where we can use E3 to pull out an issue constellation that exists within the matrix.

Issue Constellation

Here is another model of experience lamination and the connections between various emotional issues/dynamics.

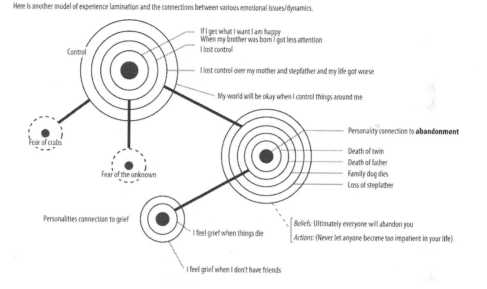

Diagram 5. *The connection between issues can happen at different layers of experiences. In this model, when we work on the death of the father, the later issues of control (i.e., fear of the unknown, fear of crabs) and grief are all resolved. This illustrates how multiple issues can resolve when harmonized.*

You will notice many concentric circles connected by lines in Diagram 5. The central circle represents the emotional dynamic and its belief system. Each additional surrounding circle represents another experience that laminated over that belief system. The diagram shows one to several circles, but in reality there may be thousands. The lines that connect the many circles are indicating a connection to a different emotional dynamic. The connecting lines can connect at various laminations from one to the other. This is shown by a line starting at the core of one concentric circle but connecting to an outer layer of another. This is where two different emotional dynamics either share the same experience or are somehow connected through each issue's belief system

My favorite dog story explains the idea of issue constellations very well. One of my good friends got a new puppy when his old dog died. He took the new dog down to the beach, where they played catch. When they got home, he rinsed and dried the dog before coming into the house. This all went like clockwork for several months. The beach was a fun place for both the dog and the owner. Soon the dog realized that every time my friend brought out the leash, they were going to the beach. Life was good. This is a classic example of a conditioned response. Leash comes out and dog jumps up and down waiting for the fun to begin. Laminations are forming around the beach with a connection to the leash and thus the leash is fun. Concentric circles are forming with connections early on between the leash and the beach. Well, one day when man and dog returned from the beach, the dog received his usual bath. However, during the bath, a large trash truck rumbled creating a huge noise and the ground even shook. The dog became very frightened and ran away at which point my friend became angry and demanded the dog return. But the dog did not return, hid under the house and refused to come out for quite a while. The dog finally calmed down and all seemed to be fine.

The next day when they returned from the beach, the dog ran underneath the house when my friend turned on the hose. The dog had now connected the water to the fear of the loud screeching, rumbling, earthshaking noise. My friend eventually coaxed the puppy out and got him washed up. But at the end of this, the dog was still very nervous. Imagine if my friend had, in his frustration, punished the dog or failed to take extra care to comfort him after the bath. The issue would have become laminated and more resolute. Luckily for both of them my friend instantly got the connection and helped to reconstruct new positive associations that diminished the pattern of fear that was created by the garbage truck. This is a very clear example of how issue constellations are formed.

Harmonization is the next step in the E3 process. It is the process of bringing two parts or two ideas into alignment and part of this process is examining the fundamental belief life can be controlled by our actions. Commonly, we must revisit past situations and re-create them and look at them through a present day lens. This is accomplished through mini-hypnotherapy sessions which can break addictions to certain behaviors or change conditioned responses. The goal is to change how a patient engages with the sensitizing event, and to help integrate new behaviors. Patients require insight to see and know that what they are doing in their life now is not working and that they must change their beliefs to change their reactions. The more the new response is repeated, the more dedicated patients are to the new path.

Additionally, people can change their action to help change their beliefs. The new actions must be very different from the old patterns and if a person is struggling with what the new action should be, it is in all likelihood the polar opposite of the dysfunctional action. When a person does the opposite of their conditioned behavior, they will directly engage their fears. The E3 process creates a new response habit that is free of fear, a new evolving, positive life path. This is the evolution of E3.

Now let's look at the deconstruction and reconstruction phase that occurs as we harmonize emotional issues. The E3 process leads the practitioner to the emotional energetic issue that when harmonized, will have the greatest therapeutic value for the patient. Because of the interconnections that exist, harmonizing this issue could conceivably remove several issues at once. The process generally starts like this: the core issue and experience is the central circle. E3 begins at the first experience that sensitized the event. (There are times when I find two issues sharing the same experience, but this is not typical.) Harmonizing the more central issue allows fragment issues – those not connected to other issues – to simply disappear without doing any specific work. In the previous example of the dog, I start with the fragment issue at its central core; the dog's fear of the bath. Harmonizing this piece leads to a more central issue when I ask if there are any links or other issues to be addressed: the dog's fear of impending doom via the noisy, earth-shaking trash truck. In both of these cases, the issue constellation begins to crumble. I then employ the principles and guidelines of

E3 to harmonize the issue as well as the patient's own wisdom to reconstruct their matrix. Let's examine how this matrix comes to be.

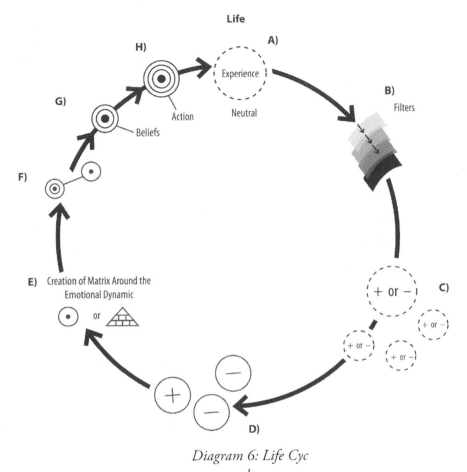

Diagram 6: Life Cyc
le

Diagram 6 illustrates how the emotional dynamic matrix is constructed. All of life's experiences begin as neutral, neither good nor bad (A). These experiences pass through several filters (B) that categorize the experiences based on the particular filter. Personality is the most powerful filter but others include your family of origin's energetic field, your society and the societal filter. The experiences are categorized, either wholly or in fragments, and given a positive or negative rating (C,D,and E). This begins the building of the emotional dynamic matrix. The experience can be connected to other emotional dynamics (F) and beliefs are established based on the experiences and filters that have categorized them in accordance with the personality's life issues (G). Finally, actions result from the beliefs (H).

The more similar experiences are categorized, the faster the cycle moves resulting in action. We no longer have to consciously think about our reactions because the actions becomes a knee jerk response. Every action is a chosen conditioned response, either unconscious or conscious.

I share another case history that illustrates this idea. I worked with a very bright and introspective patient named Susan. She was also extremely sensitive, passionate and able to fully experience all her feelings. She was also terrified of crabs and spiders.

She was afraid of their quick and erratic movements, especially if they were moving towards her and she felt that they would either bite or grab her with their claws. She also feared swimming in the ocean. This fear grew even worse if the water visibility was low. She was afraid of the countless things that might sneak up and get her, not least among them, crabs lurking under the sand or in the rocks. Consequently, she panicked whenever she was touching the ocean bottom in cloudy water. Susan was conflicted because she very much wanted to go snorkeling and swimming on warm beaches. In taking history, I learned many things about Susan's life including the fact that she had only had two significant boyfriends in her life and she was almost thirty years old. In both of those relationships, she and her partner did not live together and I had an intuitive sense that there was some blockage in regards to the need to control her space.

As Susan was getting ready for a vacation in the tropics, we started working on her fears of crabs and the murky water. I determined that the central issues concerning the crabs were: control over one's space, acceptance of one's self, and the ability to feel safe and free from harm. She would be traveling with a male friend whom she had known for several months and she really wanted to release these fears so she could enjoy her trip. She went on her vacation and happily, she returned with a great big smile on her face. I asked what had happened and she told me she was very uneasy when she arrived at the beach. The sand was filled with small holes that harbored small sand crabs and there were many larger holes that she feared housed more dangerous crabs. Because of the work we had done, she was able to tell her travel partner for the first time how she had feared the crabs and she even confided in him about

23

her fear of the water. He was able to coax her out into the water well beyond her usual limits.

For the next few days, she allowed a wide berth to the crabs and even to the holes in the sand as she walked on the beach. She had developed a sense of trust with her partner and he took his finger and put it into a hole where they had just seen a crab go. He did it more than once, and held her hand in the process. Next, he invited her to stick her finger in the hole and hold it there for five seconds. She told me she was able to count to ten. The next day her friend caught a crab and as he held it in his hand, he asked her to cover his hand with hers. They slowly rotated their hands so Susan's was on the bottom and she could feel the crab skittering all around trying to find an exit. She was able to hold her hand still with her new found strength. They lowered their hands to the ground and he removed his. The crab sat still for quite a while but eventually scurried off and Susan never pulled her hand away.

From that moment forward, everything transformed. The next day the surf became much larger and the water more turbulent with strong currents and visibility at zero. Yet Susan was out in the murky water having the time of her life, jumping through the waves.

Susan found the inner strength to face her greatest fears. And it is something we all must do - we must all hold the crab before we can move on. We must have experiences that directly conflict with our belief systems so that we learn that fear is never as big as reality.

When a new experience comes in, we give it a plus or a minus based on our personality and consciousness. Pluses and minuses for experiences on the first row of the pyramid help to develop our belief systems. On the following rows, the pluses and minuses help to fortify the belief systems. Then we replicate the action that derives from those beliefs and we continue to look for experiences that agree. We don't want to be confused by the facts. Susan walked the cycle of emotional lamination backwards. She created a different action which then caused a different belief. Once the belief system was changed, the negative was replaced by a positive. This is an important lesson. The first step is to walk into our greatest fears with open arms. Once this is done, the process of de-lamination has begun. It is akin to running the experience flywheel backwards and undoing the laminations.

Susan's emotional energetics connected crabs, cloudy and turbulent water, and loss of control all in one lamination. When she held a crab in her hand without fear, the other two issues dissolved. Soon after Susan returned from her trip, she moved in with her partner. Apparently her work with the crab was even more significant than I had realized. When people are on the path of self-discovery, elimination of their fears expands their lives much quicker than expected. Once the lamination's foundation is broken, the walls begin to crumble. Please note how multiple peripheral issues can resolve simultaneously when working on core issues. The following Diagram 7 shows us Susan's Cycle.

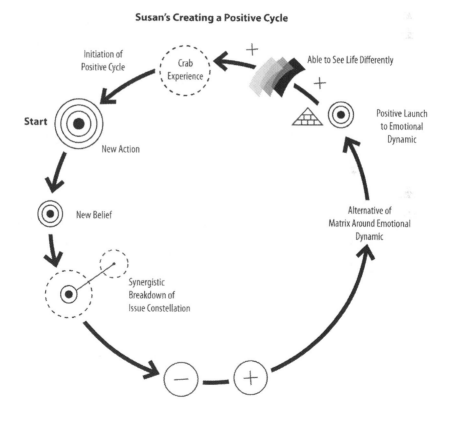

Diagram 7. Susan Creates a Positive Cycle

There are many times in life when we experience defining moments; moments and experiences that can change our life. In the beginning, we create our belief systems and develop corresponding behaviors. Then we laminate our beliefs. Defining moments are often surrounded by the fear of change. We grow used to sameness and take comfort in routine. But this is not what life is about. Many times we choose not to change because we are afraid of confronting our fears or the unknown. We must learn to discern when things need to be changed and when they do not and defining moments are opportunities to deeply enrich our life experience. Change is often bumpy with ups and downs and it is certainly the road less traveled. But it is in change where we find *life*. When I am making a decision, I pretend I am making that decision on the last day of my life. I ask myself if the decision adds richness to my existence. Does it embrace a diverse experience? Will I be harmonizing the things that cause stress or chaos, and deepening the richness of relationships? Does this give my life direction? This exercise guides me in the decision making process.

Asking whether life is directed is a very good question and one we may never find an answer to. Sometimes I feel that defining moments are pushed in front of me by my soul or by some larger force that is beyond my comprehension. I also feel this way when I examine the harmonization process. I am amazed at the opportunities to change dysfunctional belief systems. Maybe it's because human beings have a great capacity to manifest, as our greatest thought form is what we attract or create in our life. Unfortunately, let's face it; if we do one thousand things right and one thing wrong, which do we focus on? Since the vast majority of us talk more about the thing we did wrong, and more about our fears than the positive aspects of our life, it stands to reason that we are creating the things we fear.

Life taps us on the shoulder urging us to change and if we continue to ignore these taps, we get hit by the cosmic 2 x 4. We wait until the end of our lives to change when we feel time slipping away. This is definitely when we are likely to make the greatest changes in the shortest period of time as we feel we have nothing to lose and are free to say and do anything. This is when we realize how precious life is and want every moment to be free of chaos. In their last days, many people say things to family members that they've been holding on to. Two of the best weeks in my mother's and my relationship came during her final weeks.

My mother's health challenges were not over when she fought colon cancer. Years later, she was due to have a routine surgery and went in for pre-op blood work. The results showed she had an aggressive form of leukemia. I spent two weeks with her in the hospital, during which time we worked through 90% of the junk that had accumulated between us for over forty years, stuff that we had never really discussed, had been too afraid to discuss, and that had kept us from being as close as we could have been. Those two weeks contained moments of crucial honesty, humility and kindness. I wish we had done it sooner, but I'm glad it happened. During that time, my mother also extended her ability to be grounded and to experience every moment to its fullest. She took nothing for granted. Each and every fragment of every experience was expanded and transformed to a positive. She connected to everyone she met in the hospital and beliefs that had blocked living in the present moment were shattered. These were replaced by new, expanded beliefs as well as a greater feeling of community. I believe she felt the oneness that I have heard so much about.

I repeatedly see people battling life threatening dis-ease find the intensity and dedication to suck the marrow out of life. It is in the moments before death that we learn how to live. I have often wondered if we could learn this life lesson before death, would we need the dis-ease to transform us? If life is learning to *enjoy living*, then dis-ease might be the greatest teacher we have. If we found out this very moment that we had a terminal dis-ease, how would we write the final pages in our book of life? Take a moment and let this sink in. Even reading this could be a defining moment.

This is the gift of the E3 technique. Every time an emotional dynamic is harmonized it removes a filter from the kaleidoscope. Before, everything was colored with the fear of this issue. Vision expands with each filter we remove and we see life as it truly is.

These are the fundamental steps of the E3 process. Its techniques can be used by anyone – layperson or practitioner. Use it to make the decisions that lead to health and happiness. When our beliefs and so-called truths keep us from fully enjoying life, E3 facilitates the awareness to change. It provides a path and guidelines to transform experiences without creating a new set of problems, thereby removing the barriers to intuition, inner wisdom and our truest nature.

Chapter 2

THE PATH TO HARMONIZATION

THIS CHAPTER CLARIFIES THE PROCESS of how we become sensitized to certain emotional issues. We gain understanding about how to deconstruct old patterns and then reconstruct new patterns of behavior and thoughts when we understand how our emotional dynamics come to be. Our new patterns improve our health and peace of mind. This is harmonization. We never lose the core issues but as they become transformed, they change from chaos and stress inducing to gift giving.

The conscious mind is loud and easy to hear but the subconscious mind, the realm of energy and the emotions, speaks in a mere whisper. One must engage in a quiet, inward journey in order to access the emotional dynamics that are being processed in the various organs, tissues and energetic centers of the body. This is the process of self reflection and learning to find peace amidst chaos. The inward journey requires walking into one's fears and engaging with the shadow side that has been pushed into darkness. Harmonizing emotional issues and beliefs within our own unique personalities means removing the filters that keep us from accepting ourselves and those around us. The more we remove the barriers to the reality around us, the more we can access the information around us. This is the path that brings us to the limitless potential of knowledge and wisdom as well as inner peace.

A life's path is adorned with an infinite number of moments setting a dramatic backdrop for the belief systems we choose. Self-awareness reminds us of who we can be, what the harmonized path looks like and realization of how issues affect our decision making process. Transition is when we decide to change our belief system. Transformation is when we choose to face our fears and Transmutation is a when we stop attracting the experiences we needed in order to change the old fears and belief systems. This process creates an openness in our consciousness and access to greater wisdom.

A patient came to me feeling miserable and upset that nothing was going right in her life. She had seen many therapists without any resolution to her distress so I began the E3 process. Muscle tests revealed that she was processing an emotional issue. She became defensive when the issue became revealed and she immediately told me that she no longer had that issue, that she had already done the work on that issue two years ago with another therapist who determined she had worked it through. Her distress continued so she began to see another therapist. She left that therapist as well, feeling like she was getting nowhere.

The muscle testing took us right back to where the previous therapist left off as this emotional dynamic was the core issue of her life. This was such a big and tender issue that it was very difficult for her to allow it to come out of the shadows. Remember, most of us have very logical, if not honorable, reasons not to face fears. We grow used to our fears and stresses and often the most stressed people commonly don't *feel* stressed because they have no other state to compare it to. They are always stressed. People who have a noticeable spike in their stress are the ones that take notice of it and are motivated to return to a stress free state. It is usually the contrast that gives an individual the capacity to make this distinction

This woman's experience illustrates how the harmonizing emotional baggage is a process. When I asked what she had done to alter the behavior patterns regarding this issue, she did not have an answer. She had not actively kept the issue front and center in order to make changes. When this happens, the issues or symptoms may decrease for a short time, but reassert themselves later with the same vigor. The important part is not to think of harmonization as a one-time thing where the issue is discussed and then it vanishes. There is no special pill or a magic button to press to make it go away. It is a process and when one realizes and acknowledges the issues at play, this can be the gateway to change. When we get to the point where we can sniff it out every time it comes up, we are on the right path. Once we make the choice to change beliefs and the actions they motivate, then we have made lasting change.

Each person is born into this world with a basic personality, the true authentic self. Wide open, we have an almost infinite capacity to learn and adapt to the systems around us. In learning how to be from everyone and everything around us, we take on the incredible tenderness of humanity as well as its chaos. We interpret the chaos in a way that is unique to our personality and filters, integrating both the good and bad experiences. We then spend the rest of our lives harmonizing and smoothing out the rough spots.

Thus we create our own emotional matrix. We become initially sensitized to the big core issues and then create fears, the darkest shadows being formed from conception to about the age of six. These shadows are the belief systems about ourselves or our desires that we are hide from others. Remember that the core issues and shadows will follow the construction of one's beliefs and personal laws. This may lead to feelings of being socially acceptable. The years from age seven to age twelve also brew core issues of life, but the energetic treasures and sensitivities are usually found before this. The events that occur after age twelve are generally peripheral in nature.

We take the various experiences and begin to collate them, taking different events in our lives and assigning them to a range of emotional issues. One event might represent feelings of abandonment, lack of control and lack of love. As stated earlier, these emotional issues become the bottom rows of a pyramid and then there are connections formed all the way up, across and diagonally through the pyramid and sphere of our subconscious thinking.

All of us have done this. One thought leads us to another and then another. Each category of new memories is organized and interconnected in response to our life's experiences, our consciousness that is entwined with our personality, the history of our family, the wise voice of our soul and perhaps our past lives. We assign positive or negative value to the experiences and we spend our lives seeking out those positive experiences and avoiding the negative. After all, negative experiences feel bad and are often accompanied by feelings of inadequacy, fears, betrayals and worse. Unfortunately, when most people take an inventory, the negative or minus category is longer than the positive.

I recently experienced a situation where I was very angry. The angrier I became the more my leg hurt. The situation presented where I found myself feeling forced to do something I did not want to do and that the people forcing me were winning and I was losing. My ego did not like this situation at all. In this case, I knew I was right and was being extorted by a small-town bureaucracy. For two nights, I had difficulty sleeping because my leg hurt so much. I could not let go of the cyclic thoughts and the anger. Every time the thought came about, I felt the negative effects on my body. I was bathing myself in the neurochemicals of adrenaline and all those that attenuate the feelings of anger. I could feel these chemicals cascading over my entire body and the detrimental effects of this would make me more susceptible to dis-ease and aging.

I decided enough was enough. I wanted to stop the un-harmonious cycle. I had to affect my matrix so I grabbed a piece of paper and pencil and made two categories, one titled Plus and Minus. Then I began to listen to my subconscious thoughts. These are the whispers just below the conscious mind, the thoughts that we may not even be aware of in that moment. The subconscious thoughts are the constant stream of thoughts that fill the mind when we meditate. I made a checkmark in the corresponding column for every positive or negative thought that came to me. I averaged one positive thought for every nine negative ones. I had nine times as many detrimental chemicals in my body as I did good ones. This had to stop! Every time I sensed a negative subconscious thought, I went to its roots to determine why it was negative. A common theme arose revolving around my sense of self-esteem. So I began to tear apart these belief systems to which I had become sensitized, and which I had laminated over the years. The beliefs I held so dear regarding my self-esteem were unimportant compared to my health and inner sense of peace. They had to be reframed and harmonized.

In order to change my beliefs and resulting behaviors, I needed to pull at the roots, not prune the upper branches. I had to start at the foundation of the pyramid not just with the symptoms. Working with surface symptoms will only guarantees that the work will be superficial and the issue will return. If you take the top stone block off of a pyramid, the pyramid is still standing. If change is to really occur in the matrix, we must disassemble and then reconstruct the pyramid from the base up.

This is actually great news because the experiences at the bottom of the matrix are much easier to transform than the ones on top. The ones on the top are a result of thousands, if not hundreds of thousands, of experiences that we have repeated in our life. No matter how many times an individual works with the top block it will just reconstruct itself. All the decisions, plusses and minuses, beliefs, and actions that are the foundations of the top block still exist. The higher up the pyramid, the more resolute and rigid the beliefs. The foundational blocks on the bottom, however, are soft and unsupported by other events. These are much easier to work with.

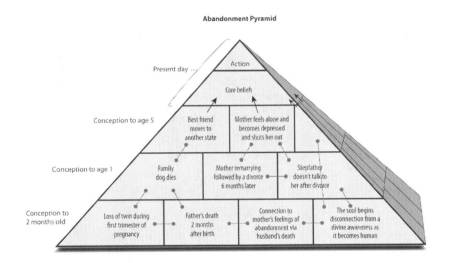

Diagram 8. Abandonment Pyramid. At the apex of the pyramid are the actions that are the ultimate result of the beliefs formulated from life experiences. The emotional issue/dynamic will be determined by that personality. The person's personality will filter and transform all of life's events to be seen in way that it conforms to and activates their core issues.

Here's even better news. The moment we transform a block on the bottom row, the pyramid begins to crumble. Instantly everything re-associates and reconstitutes itself as everything above the first row is compensation to the initial sensitizing events and the beliefs that they create. Each person will see things through the filter of their personality.

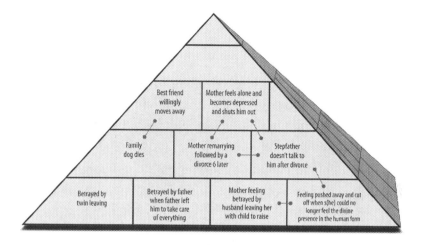

Diagram 9. Betrayal Pyramid. Different personalities with catalogue the same life experiences into different emotional dynamics because the person is hardwired differently. Different personalities will have different sensitivity to feel betrayed by the same experience.

The two-dimensional pyramid holds within it one major sensitized belief system, in this case abandonment. Belief system pyramids become aligned , tips all pointing towards each other. One of the pyramids next to abandonment might be grief or loneliness and there may be positive pyramids adjoined as well. It could relate to friendship or love. These pyramids together create the infinitely faceted geodesic sphere, a very strong interrelated collection of the person's beliefs, that dictate all of the actions in his or her life.

Our personality and consciousness predisposes us to see things a certain way. We also grasp certain issues that our personality resonates with, the things you are meant to harmonize in your life. The first row of pyramid blocks are laid down and the experience is assigned a value judgment. The next time a similar experience occurs, we look for the category in which it belongs and then put the new experience, as a block, on top of the fully formed first row. If this experience was previously deemed positive (given a 'plus'), the body manufactures the neurochemicals or drugs that are associated with that category. A plus experience creates neurochemistry that makes us feel good. These neurochemicals are either secreted into the bloodstream by glands or are made by individual cells within our body. Some cells and organs can produce more neurochemicals than others but nearly all the cells of our body have receptor sites for these neurochemicals. Again, some tissues have more receptor sites than others. The musckulosketal, neurological, digestive, vascular and immune systems are most intimately connected to these neurochemicals.

Some of the better-known neurochemicals are endorphins and enkephalins. These morphine - like chemicals are powerful positive reinforcers. One hit from these and we will want more and once our body figures out this positive response, we spend the rest of our life trying to find a way to get these chemicals to release. There are lots of different neurochemicals that give rise to the multitude of different feelings that we have. The negative chemicals on the other hand give us feelings that we wish to escape or avoid.

Psychologists have frequently pondered the question of nurture versus nature, our experiences versus our innate qualities. I believe it is important to go even further and divide nature into two components: physical things and energetic components that we cannot measure objectively. Let's begin with a newborn who comes into this world with a physical and an energetic body. The energetic body contains the blueprint of our physical form, the precursor of physicality. The energetic body also includes the consciousness, subconscious, memories and soul. An example can be seen in Kirlian photography.

Diagram 10. Kirlian Hands. Photo from www.wholetruthsolutions.com

Kirlian photography is a form of high voltage electro-photography that images the energetic body. This picture shows two normal hands with the energetic imprint of the hands. But if someone were to have their hands amputated, the energetic outline of the hand would still be seen using this type of photography. Also, if the person were experiencing pain in the hand prior to the amputation, the hand pain would persist post amputation. There is no physical explanation for this, but there certainly is an energetic one. The following example is a good illustrator of this phenomenon. I was teaching Qi Gong to a class and a student called to report that he would not be coming back to class as he had severely burned his hand in a grease fire. His doctors were recommending partial amputation of his hand. The burn had removed all of his skin and most of the muscle in parts of his hand. He asked my opinion. I told him to push energy from his well hand into the injured hand and when he did this, he still felt energy in the injured hand as if it was all there. I believed that as long as he could feel energy in the injured hand, muscle and skin grafts would be successful so he should hold off on the amputation. I did some distance energy work with him, imagining my work on his hand. Though he lived thousands of miles away, he could feel exactly where I was working on his hand and could confirm the direction and pattern of my hand movements. He continued this same work himself three to five times a day and continued even after the skin grafts were in place. Much to the surprise of his medical doctors, the grafts were a success and his hand returned to normal function. These cases confirm that physicality and energetics are intimately interconnected and coexist. Even though we cannot see the energetic realm with our eyes, we can feel the results of its existence.

Another example of an energetic realm of consciousness is instinct. The knowledge and experience of countless generations makes up instinct but it cannot be shown to be passed from generation to generation physically. We know it exists but how is this information transmitted?

The animal kingdom gives us some insight.

In one study on migratory birds, specifically geese, researchers took eggs from nests on the east coast of the United States and swapped them with eggs from nests on the west coast. When the goslings hatched, the baby birds were tagged. The researchers found that when the goslings were ready to take flight, they flew cross-country to return to their native flyways. They traversed directly back to their respective flyways without the help of their parents and seemed to follow the historical landmarks to guide them to their southern wintering grounds. These were baby birds without previous experience but still they carried with them the experiences of those before them, possessing a piece of energetic consciousness that guided them on their journey. We find another example with fish such as salmon and steelhead. These anadromous fish return to the same exact spot in the river where they were born to spawn. How could they do this if not for some download to their consciousness? What tells them that their very survival depends on returning to a stream tributary that will support them through their gestation? All of us have seen animals give birth and instinctively know how to care for their young. The interplay between the energetic realms of consciousness and the realms of our perceivable physicality are beyond any paradigm we can conceive.

These animal examples highlight the role of the energetic subconscious and how it receives input. We need open minds to explore the co-creation of our energetic consciousness, our physical being, and the role these play in our own emotional dynamics.

Consciousness is the end result of input from both energetic and physical sources and it is quite possible that DNA carries within it information from both sources. Each parent provides an equal amount of DNA, combined to provide all the information for growth and development. We are born with a unique personality but that personality if often like one or both of our parents. The roots of personality can be found in the family tree, which is interesting if we study emotional issues that follow the family line. Most people have heard the biblical quotation, "The Lord visits the iniquity of the fathers on the children and on the grandchildren to the third and fourth generations " (Exodus 34:6-7). This is oft interpreted as the sins of the parents becoming the sins of the children. The Hebrew word for sin, "Chet," is actually an archery term meaning "to miss the mark." This is quite different from thinking of sin as committing some shameful offense. So we can understand the Bible to teach that these generational sins of families miss the target of unconditional love. For example, if your family has historically struggled with being good enough or self–acceptance, there will often be a lot of judgment and guilt used in the family dynamics. These issues become passed on from parents to children so that each generation deals with the same issues in their life and time. The issues that each of us work on can come from our broad family tree.

In just five generations, you can have input from 64 relatives. In ten generations this increases to 2,048 relatives. Travel fifteen generations back and you have input from 63,488 relatives. So don't despair if a particular issue has been in your family for 15 generations. You have had the company of 63,488 relatives working on this issue along with you and you receive the benefit of the work that they have done throughout their lives. Your job is to smooth out any residual emotional dynamics that remain.

This logarithmic exercise is to remind us that issues can come from a multitude of places and that we are part of something that has great depth. The medical name for this connecting phenomenon is simply familial tendencies. The homeopathic term for this is a miasm. The energetic component of these issues is called a familial field effect. Talk to your relatives and ask them, "What were the things that caused the greatest stress in your life?" You may be able to save yourself a lot of time getting to the core issue and getting on the path to understanding yourself.

An employee of mine had a familial history of breast cancer. She herself was diagnosed with breast cancer in her 30s and she subsequently decided to have a bilateral mastectomy. She was well aware of the depth of her familial tendency, and she planned her health decision accordingly. In another example, a friend had a family history of all the men contracting lung cancer. We assume that lung cancer is caused by smoking or other chemical exposure but none of these men smoked and none of them were exposed to carcinogenic chemicals that would predispose them. This man died in middle age from the dis-ease as had the other men in his family before him.

The medical model for these familial cancers is that there is an oncogene, a gene in the familial DNA that presdisposes us to a specific cancer. This gene can cause cells to become malignant and run wild when the person comes into contact with a certain chemical or carcinogen or virus. This may be the cause in some cases but I believe the roots of many familial dis-eases are more energetic in nature. The reason for familial diseases including cancer is still unfolding. There are many recorded instances where people with strong family dispositions towards certain dis-eases adopt children from foreign countries who then become prone to the same dis-eases. It appears that the younger the adoptee, the stronger these connections are. This indicates at least anecdotally that there is something happening other than genetics within family energetic fields. This is called the proximal familial energetic field.

Familial Energetic Field

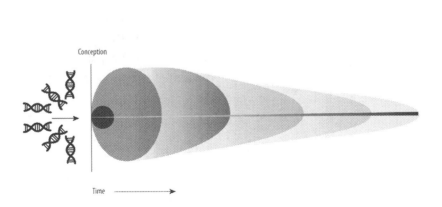

Diagram 11. Familial Energetic Field.

The effect is wider and has greater influence in the early parts of life and less influence as we get older. As we age, we individuate and deal with

38

our emotional issues as well as receive more and more input from those outside of the family. The proximal field is comprised of the relatives that you share similar DNA therefore you will have more connection with them. The closer your DNA is, the more you will be able to communicate energetically. This means you may share their lessons and belief systems. There is also a distal field meaning relatives far back on the family tree can still affect the emotional dynamics. Past life experiences can also affect your consciousness. Looking for the initial sensitizing event can lead me to past life experiences. It can take more than one life to work through certain emotional issues and a person may be on the second or third life working on alternative views and experiences for the same issue. Many of us have either had or known people who have had recollections of past lives.

As practitioners, it is essential that we entertain past life dynamics as a possible starting point for initial sensitizing events. It may not matter if you personally believe in past lives or not to do this work. One of my chiropractic colleagues raised in a devout Christian family engages with this concept as precognition, as an experience we are connected to prior to birth. Past lives could be the lives of other people, maybe someone in our family tree. If nothing else, realize the invaluable therapeutic result that will come when working with the initial event, whether it is in this present life or a past life.

I ask questions to determine whether or not past life experiences are at play. These questions may include how many lifetimes ago (or years ago if preferred), on which continent the life was lived, or what was your gender. I usually find the initial sensitizing event began within the past ten lives. If it goes farther back than that, it is likely that the person lived several lives where they did not work on this particular issue. They may have jumped to a different issue based on their circumstances and the people they lived with, but they are now re-engaging in harmonizing the original issue. I also ask about the personality they manifested in the past life. This will make more sense later after reading about personality. Personalities give great clues to the issues and struggles of that life. It is also possible that they moved away from one particular issue because they changed personalities and wrestled with different issues. For more information on past lives I strongly recommend the book, <u>Destiny of Souls</u> by Michael Newton, Ph.D.

It is truly amazing to think of how many lives we may have already experienced. Human beings used to have children before they were twenty-years-old. If humanity has been around for 50,000 years, there is the potential for having lived 2,500 lives. This number might be high as there are often breaks between lives, but there are also instances when people die at a very young age. What a great system this is to allow us so many chances to work through an issue until it is harmonized. Then we can move on to the next issue that needs to be experienced and harmonized. If we think we are going to finish working on our issues and be done coming back to the physical world, guess again. As practitioners, we will witness the great depth of input from past lives. It is a founding principle of all psychological work that we start at the beginning of the issue or it will keep coming back.   Besides familial and past life input, we also may receive information from humanity's group consciousness or what I will call the soul. This is the little voice that directs us in many of our daily events as well as the larger defining moments of our lives. All these things represent the possible origins of where we receive the energetic input.

<u>Groundhog Day</u> was one of the most psychologically astute films ever made about laminating the psychological experience. In the 1993 movie by Harold Ramis, the main character Phil (played by Bill Murray) repeats the same day over and over again. Every day he repeats the same actions. A situation comes up which reminds us of a previous event and we employ the designated response for that stimulus. The response is based on a previously generated belief and voilà, life becomes like the movie Groundhog Day .

Phil is trapped in his own personal purgatory, even attempting suicide several times. Some people would rather die than change. Some aspects of our belief system actually must die before transformation occurs. Phil finally reaches a crisis point and does change his beliefs about himself and the world around him. In that moment, he shatters the old laminations and begins to create a harmonious, flourishing life.

It's hard to say why we follow a set stimulus response protocol instead of seeing each situation as unique. We catalog our life experiences, laminating them into beliefs. The more laminations we create, the more addicted we are to the belief system and the resulting actions. However, certain beliefs are dysfunctional so if we don't listen to the little voice requesting change, we get hit with the cosmic 2 x 4. Hopefully, a 2 x 4 is enough motivation to change.

There are seven landmarks on the path to harmonization. The first hallmark is a dysfunctional belief system. The beliefs may have served us at one time in our lives but the system can become dysfunctional and create chaos and emotional stress. This is an invitation to change what no longer serves us but sometimes it takes a stronger motivator, what I call a cosmic 2 x 4, like pain or hardship or dis-ease to really get us to change our lives. The most common of dis-eases associated with emotional stress are skin ailments, stomach conditions, chronic musculoskeletal symptoms, ulcerative colitis and irritable bowel syndrome, heart arrhythmias, high blood pressure, eating disorders, and autoimmune diseases. This list is long and is by no means all inclusive. If dysfunctional belief systems and the issues they bring about are not dealt with over time, the body begins to break down and the life force is chronically inhibited. Superficial diseases can morph into more serious diseases because the natural healing ability of the body is impaired. Dis-ease ensues but not without warning. A person usually experiences countless frustrations, disappointments, anger, delusions and repeated confrontations with the emotional issues at hand. They usually feel exhausted. Dis-ease is the last ditch effort to wake us up. I do want to repeat that I do not believe that all dis-ease comes from and emotional source. But there is almost always an emotional component to every dis-ease we encounter.

The second landmark is awakening. I describe this as the lucid moment where we truly see life as it is, not through the lens of past belief systems. Awakening is when we see the problem or the issue clearly and also see why our previous beliefs and actions did not resolve it. Awakening creates a great opening and healing and invigorates us with new energy. The downside is that despite this sure of insight, people will actually have a relapse in struggling with the issue at hand. Why? Because we say, "I feel great. Maybe the problem is not that bad after all and I don't really need to change." We are presented with the opportunity to return to the familiar, dysfunctional ways. The good news is that even if we revert to the old behaviors, the universe is very patient and will once again provide the experiences that invite us to change. The cycle will begin again and exhaustion and frustration will happen again. Awakening once makes it easier to wake up again and each time we experience the shift, we move a little closer towards resolving what previously caused chaos.

The following diagram shows these landmarks along the process of harmonizing an emotional issue. Please note that as we visit these different stages, we reconfigure our belief systems. You can see that the line representing this path gets thinner and thinner as we move through the process. This indicates that the issue becomes smaller and smaller. Our core issues never go away, but they can become so small that they no longer cause us to leap into the old actions. Rather, they will serve only to remind us of the great work we have done.

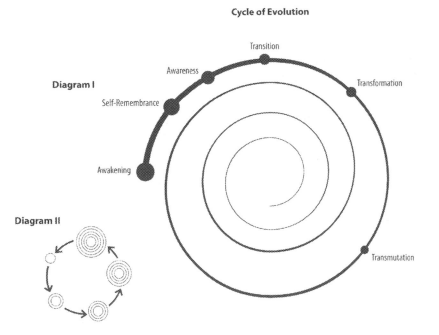

Diagram 12.

Each trip around the cycle deconstructs one more layer that keeps us addicted to an old behavior.

The third landmark on the path to harmonization is self–remembrance. This is when we remember what we were like before and who we could be without this dysfunctional belief. This step has many layers of understanding and learning and it is an essential part of "becoming" who we are truly meant to be. We can envision feeling peaceful despite being surrounded by chaos. As we deepen our self–remembrance, we will shatter the false illusions and find out who we really are: a radically unique self.

Landmark four is awareness. We become aware when we can examine an emotional issue, its associated beliefs and behaviors, and acknowledge its influence on our life. For example, look at the emotional dynamic of judgment. If one is overly judgmental, awareness happens when we can examine how we benefit from the ego actively lifting itself up, while putting others down. The judgmental ego relishes seeing others fail or do poorly because comparisons allow us to hide from the fear of not being good enough. We become aware of how many times a day we exhibit judgmental behavior. As our awareness deepens, we soon realize that judgment seeps into our decision making, speech, body language, and generally feeling smug and superior towards others. Soon we realize that thousands of thoughts in our day pass through the judgment filter and our actions are tainted with the dysfunctional belief system of hierarchy and righteousness. Without awareness of this dysfunction, we cannot change.

The fifth landmark is transition. Once we awaken to the issues, remember who we truly are and become aware of the problem, we have climbed up to the very peak of the mountain of change. Now we stand, one foot on the slope we have ascended and the other foot on the downhill side of this issue. This is the defining point where we make a decision to fall back down into the abyss or venture forward down the slopes of re-creation and the unknown. We have done the hardest work, becoming aware of the emotional dynamics at play and choosing change. The rest of the journey is much easier as we decide what to believe and what our actions will be. Once we resolve to move forward, we move seamlessly from transition into transformation.

Transformation is the sixth landmark., the exciting time when we re-create ourselves guided by life lessons and experiences. We increase our ability to hear the inner voice of wisdom when we remove emotional filters. It is still difficult to bring this consciousness to awareness because it is masked by the insistent drone of the ego and the emotional issues of our past, yet this inner voice represents the true self. Our true identity moves to the forefront when the urgency of the narcissistic ego is halted. It is here that we see the oneness of all things and how we are within, and a part of an immense creation. As the weight of the emotional issues is removed, we are propelled forward to continue the process.

Transformation is coupled with transmutation, the seventh landmark, as the energetic and physical restructuring of one's self takes place. The matrix of our being, which has been defragmented, is reconfigured during this stage. It is the new self that believes differently, acts differently, looks and feels differently. Each of these stages gives a wonderful energetic push as we are released from the bondage of old chaotic patterns. Each step brings us closer to freedom.

Chapter 3

PERSONALITY AND COLORS

I RECEIVE CONSISTENT FEEDBACK FROM the attendees at my seminars about the value of learning about personality in the process of self-discovery. Students know something is not working in their lives and they want to change but because they live with themselves and their behaviors day in and day out, they don't know where to start. It's hard to pick out the specific issues that need to be resolved. Learning about personality provides insights into ourselves as well as those around us. This knowledge often shines a bright light on the issues and hurdles in life that trip us up.

We are not isolated in the challenges we face. People who share personality traits wrestle with the same issues. Awareness and self discovery opens doors to the journey of all those that share a certain personality. In a seminar setting, people begin to connect with others navigating the same issues and we can cheer on each other's strengths, the things that have made us who we are in the present, as well as commiserate over the struggles we face.

The seminar setting sometimes feels like an Alcoholics Anonymous meeting. "Hi, my name is Jane. I am a Green personality. I am loving, passionate and exciting. I am working on the issue of needing to be the center of the universe and my intense need for immediate gratification of my desires. It's true, I want it all." All the other Green personality types applaud, for they all know what it is to be Green. This acceptance and understanding of the struggle gives us the strength and impetus to move through the process of harmonizing our life. This is how we grow. This is how we make peace from our chaos.

There are four main personality types, each of them represented by a color. The color is not arbitrary but represents the wavelength that the body gives off generated by the thought patterns of that personality type. This phenomenon was first identified by people who can see auras, the subtle luminosity surrounding a person. We can now correlate these findings with instrumentation that picks up electromagnetic frequencies. The basic colors are red, orange, yellow and green but there can be other colors in the aura as well such as blue, purple, and magenta. These colors reflect the standard colors that are attributed to the seven chakras of the body. The first four colors are basic personalities and the other colors reflect how we relate to our access our inner wisdom. If someone is doing the spiritual and emotional work of a life, they tend to display more of the blue,purple and magenta spectrum. People who show more blue in their aura tend to be more extroverted in nature. Blue represents the voice of the soul. Purple and magenta correlate more to introverts that spend a great deal of time on an inward journey feeling the emotions and feelings of the soul.

Each personality not only sees the world through a unique, preordained filter but each personality strives to emulate certain archetypes and embody certain emotional issues. Carl Jung described an archetype as the pattern from the collective experience that lives in the unconscious. Examples are the Rebel, the Caretaker, and the Warrior. Each personality has a set of rules with which it complies.

Each person has aspects of every personality color and traits but in different proportions. One person might be 80% Green, 10% Yellow 5% Orange and Red. This person will look and act differently from a person who is 50% Green, 40% Yellow and % Orange and Red. These behavior trends are in addition to all of the things that we inherit including our (past) life's experiences, our family experiences, familial energetic field input, and society's input. Throughout our life, this rich, internal tapestry continuously shapes and reshapes who we are.

Personality type can also be correlated to brain function. People who perceive the world through the left lateral side of their brain find the world very different than those who are right brained people. Those who process information primarily through the left frontal portions of the brain come up with completely different ways of solving problems and coping than those who primarily process in the right frontal lobes of the brain. The side of the brain that we use forecasts our beliefs and actions, and influences the development of our personal laws.

What is it like to be right-brained versus left-brained? Some of the personalities don't just bias one side of the brain but start on one side and then change over to the other. Simply put, human beings are truly processing centers. We perceive incoming stimuli which we then sort and categorize using the stored information in our memories, but the process always goes through the personality filter. Then we respond based on our personality and belief systems. Each of these steps, perception and response, is dictated by the part of the brain we use. In addition, every cell in our body also has a memory and has input in this perception and response process.

The parts of the brain that are most intensely involved in perception include the limbic system, and the parietal lobes. The occipital and temporal lobes, which are involved in sight and hearing are involved to a lesser degree. The limbic center helps to regulate much of our bodies output, maintenance, and emotional and physical homeostasis. The hypothalamus and pituitary glands are part of the limbic system which is centrally located and provides input to both sides of the brain. The hypothalamus, though the size of a pea, regulates eating, drinking, sleeping, walking, body temperature, chemical balance, heart rate, hormones, sex drive, and emotions. This gland is often thought of as a starting place for neurochemical secretions that communicate with other organs such as the pituitary glands, adrenal glands and so on. Knowing this, it is becomes easy to understand that what we are feeling or thinking can greatly influence any of the body's functions. The thalamus gland is another structure in the center of the brain. With a lobe on each side of the brain, the thalamus helps to initiate consciousness and make preliminary classifications of external information. The basal ganglia also sit one on each side, and are very proximal to the limbic system. They perform the function of increasing adaptability. This is where decision-making, organization of the world and our individual experiences take place. It is a part of the system that holds memory and aids in producing and understanding speech. It is where paintings are seen and music is heard. The parietal lobes are intimately involved in perceiving touch and movement. They carry some of the special abilities of touch such as stereognosis, graphism and proprioception.

Proprioception is the ability to sense one's movements and placement in space. This is also where we seem to assemble our world. It is likely that this is where letters come together as words and words are put together in thoughts. This is the point of translation where our emotions, our wishes and needs also get transformed into thoughts. The left parietal lobe specializes in language, math, and writing. The right parietal lobe specializes in mental images and spatial relationships. The upper middle part of the brain is the sensory cortex and the motor cortex. These are involved in sensing our emotions and creating movement. The stimuli of smell comes through the frontal lobe but the vast majority of the frontal lobe has to do with processing, not perceiving.

This is a classic look at how the different lobes in our mind function. The right and left sides of the brain work completely differently from one another and this is why they are separated. They are like the odd couple. They have distinct manners, belief systems, personalities, and ways of looking at and organizing the world. Each perceives the world correctly but they each perceive different aspects of the same world. It is interesting that without this duality and opposition in our brain, we could not have survived.

Our left brain keys in on the physical realm through the five senses. This is essential as we are physical beings living in a physical world. The left brain processes things in a serial fashion, one step at a time, in a linear progression, via physical things that can be measured. If information doesn't come through one of these five senses, it does not exist to the left brain. It is very difficult, if not outright threatening for a left-brained person to hear a right brained person speak about intuition, inner knowledge, or universal consciousness. Perhaps one of the biggest differences is that the left side of our brains sees us solely as individuals whereas the right brain sees everything as one interconnected being. Right brainers like doing things in groups, or by consensus, whereas left brainers like to be more self-sufficient, responsible for their own selves, and are much better at doing things on their own. They are okay being alone because they see themselves as separate and distinct from others.

The right brain senses the energy world and the universal connection between all living things. This energy includes thoughts, emotions, and all life force. Energy is what intra-creates matter meaning that the two are one in the same, just different forms of the same. In other words, you can make energy out of matter and matter out of energy. Our world is made up of both and we are also energy, consciousness or spiritual beings housed in physical bodies. The right side of our brain is set up to perceive this energetic world. But this perception is also entangled with, and superimposed on the physical world. The right side of the brain helps us to function and survive in this world. Those who use the right side of their brain are strong with *The Force*, to coin a Star Wars phrase. The more we use the right brain, the more we look like Jedi masters.

Right-brainers are intuitive and have the ability to easily manifest things into the physical world. This is a profound survival skill. There are many times when logic can lead to a detrimental decision but if we trust an energetic heart decision, the one that we know intuitively to be sound, it usually serves us better than logical decisions. If you are in the middle of the desert and only see sand in all directions, the right brain will lead to water the quickest. I remember reading the daily logs of the Lewis and Clark expedition when they were at Fort Mandan in North Dakota. Everyone had run out of supplies and the buffalo had not been seen for months. Lewis and Clark witnessed a call for prayer from the Native Americans requesting that Brother Buffalo come and help sustain their tribe. The Native Americans called for three days and on the third day the buffalo showed. The expedition killed what they needed and thanked the buffalo as they prayed and wished well-being to the souls of those animals.

The right side of the brain gives us our instinct. This is the knowledge that allows a new mother to innately know how to give birth and rear her child. It is the little voice of wisdom that knows the way. We do not need a physical organ on our body to collect this information; it is an intrinsic part of us. It is very interesting that the surgical treatment to stop the grand mal seizures in patients sometimes requires large areas of either the right or left side of the brain to be disconnected from the rest. Doctors found that people can survive without the left side of the brain, but they cannot survive without the right.

Right-brain dominant people have a deep understanding that all is one. The right side of the brain is a parallel processor, which means it is made to look at everything at one time. It conceives the big picture and complex thought forms and communicates with pictures, emotional thought forms, and metaphors. It is focused on the present moment. This leads to many lessons in life about learning patience. The right brain exists in a limitless world of complete freedom where anything is possible. Without linear flow, time moves backwards just as easily as forward. This side of the brain allows us to feel another's energy with our hands, as well as pick up someone's vibe. The right side of the brain has difficulty seeing and understanding physical boundaries and barriers because of its all-is-one perception.

The left brain is made to function and survive in the physical world. This means it understands the external environment through smell, sight, hearing, touch and taste. The left brain works best in the macro world of physicality, the world of collapsing probabilities and specialization. Energy goes from a generalized form and becomes specialized as it forms the building blocks of matter or dedicated energy. The left-brain world contains individuated things that are substantial and real, with specific boundaries so left-brained people are much better at seeing the boundaries and realities of the physical world. Their world is much more literal and black-and-white. Because they see things as individualistic and separate, they are better at being alone but this is relative because all of us are social by nature. We all wish to be connected and left-brain perceivers connect through family, and groups such as sports, clubs, work and church.

Left-brainers endeavor to be self-made and enjoy a struggle, if not a battle. Their motto might be "survival of the fittest" or "if it doesn't kill you it makes you stronger." If they get knocked down, they learn how to get back up and be strong. They strongly dislike drama or anything weak because weakness is failure. The left brain survives through the greatest adversity and is the reason that humanity exists. The left brain looks for something to fear and as soon as it finds it, strategizes to eliminate or dominate it by lifting itself up and pushing others down. The sweetest nectar for a pure left-brainer is to completely control anything harmful. Because the left brain does not automatically know how to share, these individuals exhibit strong survival skills with an ability to protect themselves and their family. Strictly speaking, the left-brain doesn't want to help unless exchanging assistance for future safety. The left brain spends its life ensuring its survival through conflict.

The left brain does not speak in metaphor or in expansive philosophical terms but speaks directly, in definitive concrete terminology, which eliminates guess work. The left brain excels at writing instruction manuals or giving directions, and has difficultly writing or interpreting love poems. This brain perceives and defines its actions in linear timelines with the past in every decision, and all decisions are about future. This makes left-brained-perceiving people very traditional and conservative. Left-brainers are also very detail oriented and they know the steps from A to Z, which makes them excellent at fixing things. They enjoy taking things apart and putting them back together again so that they understand the process. This also brings a comforting sense of accomplishment. The left brain likes to live by rules and the concepts of hierarchy where all things are not created equal.

As with the right side of the brain, left-brain processing occurs primarily in the frontal lobes with input from the "mody." "Mody" is the combination of "mind" and "body, " reminding us that the two are inseparable and function as a whole. Whatever the mind is thinking, the cells in the bottom of our little toe are connected to those thoughts and to the entire process. However, the information will have been correlated and categorized, using the past, the need to function, survival, and the belief that they stand alone. Left-brainers have an infinite capacity to learn societal beliefs and use them to rank itself against others. People who perceive and process via the left brain create logical theories about separateness and hierarchy. This side of the brain says we must earn our way to the top. Only by getting to the top will we receive respect. The hierarchical left brain insists that people are better than others by virtue of what they have achieved and attained. People are either looked up to or looked down on. Yet, this wish for respect gives humanity the drive to thrive.

Left-brainers calculate an individual's scores based on societal values. The left side is the home of the ego. Not only does it perform rankings, it has a keen eye to know when it is winning or losing. Life is a constant game of comparison and it is in the left hemisphere where this contrived contest takes place. The ego thrives on contests like a close-scoring football game to see which team struggles to the top. Because of this drive, we get up every morning to go to work, stick to a schedule, eat breakfast, create order through laws, and make sure that we have a savings account and a fire extinguisher. It's the side that makes us work hard, stay physically fit, and clean and presentable. The left brain pushed us to survive as a race, yet at the same time it is the place where we hold resentment for others who disagree with us. It is the place that creates shame, blame, guilt, embarrassment, revenge, bigotry, fear, intolerance, fundamentalist ideology and even war. Because of the infinite information for the left brain to process, it is constantly working. It represents the majority of the constant chatter in our minds. Human survival depended upon one brain with the capacity to interact and succeed in both the physical and energetic worlds, and whether this was orchestrated by the Creator, or by evolution, this dual-brain system works.

Dr. Jill Bolte Taylor is an accomplished neuroanatomist who has devoted her life to studying how the brain works. She gave us an unprecedented understanding of this when she suffered a severe hemorrhage in the left hemisphere of her brain in 1996. Instead of performing an experiment cutting off blood flow to the brain in a laboratory animal, she crawled inside of her own test tube and wrote a personal memoir titled My Stroke of Insight: A Brain Scientist's Personal Journey (published in 2008 by Viking Penguin). Dr. Jill described her view of the world as the left side of her brain turned off and on as a result of the hemorrhage. I recommend her precise, insightful story to those who want to understand how personality is a reflection of which side of the brain they are using at that moment. In 2008, Dr. Jill presented her story at the TED Conference in Monterey, California. This is what I gleaned from her presentation.

When the hemorrhage was first occurring she was on an exercise machine. She looked down at her hands and body and saw them as primitive. This was when the right brain was functioning but the left brain was not. This makes me wonder if we always see ourselves as primitive when viewing through the right brain. It may hint to the fact that the consciousness that we are part of is a much more advanced being and does not require such appendages. At that point, Dr. Jill could still hear an internal voice telling the body what to do, which meant that the left brain was still functioning on some level but when she looked at her body, she was unable to determine its boundaries because the atoms and molecules of her arm blended with the atoms and molecules of her surroundings. She also noted that the constant mind chatter had stopped and she focused on the magnificence around her. Without the boundary of the body, she felt enormous, and at one with all of the surrounding energy and beauty.

The right side of the brain operates in the world of quantum mechanics where the building blocks of matter are energy. Everything is made of energy and the smaller matter is, the more it is seen as energetic rather than physical. Physicality denotes that things have boundaries, inertia, and are solid. Physicality hardens the more we view it, acknowledge it or perhaps want it to solidify. In other words, our thoughts and consciousness catalyze energy into becoming matter. The left brain struggles with invisible things such as consciousness. Looking through the right brain and the creation process of matter, we might have to expand our thoughts about what is considered alive and what is not. Through the perception of the right brain all things are interacting, adapting and giving birth via transformation, if not creation.

In the next moment, the left side of Dr. Jill's brain began to function again and said, "We have a problem. We need help." The left brain was doing its job to help her survive alerting her to danger but she once again drifted back into right-brained consciousness. The mind chatter stopped again and she reflected on how all the relationship stress had disappeared, and how beautiful and perfect relationships were now. She also felt peacefully expansive.

This reveals how the left side of the brain keeps tabs on winning and losing, not to mention resentment, which are both ego-based. Dr. Jill's left brain gave her moments of clarity that allowed her to save herself even though it was so impaired that she was unable to speak intelligibly or understand what other people were saying. When the right brain was functioning and the left was not, she had difficultly conceiving how she could squeeze this enormous consciousness back into her little body. She sensed that everyone was really whole, equal as one and that everything was in place. She talked about being in a state of nirvana and understanding that with our two cognitive minds, humans *are* the life force and power of the universe. She talked about how we had the choice to perceive and live our lives as one with all that is, or as the consciousness of an individual, solid and separate from the flow.

Dr. Jill's experience has not only given us great insights into brain personality function, but to the potential of humanity. This confirms that the left brain represents the ego, individuality, good or bad, and black-or-white and it creates the illusion so we can function and survive in the physical world. The right side may not be logical, but it is filled with wisdom. The right brain has much greater insight into the inner workings of our world. This characteristic understanding of our inner world can easily be attributed to our soul. Keeping in mind the oneness understood by the right brain, this soul is the connection point to life's collective consciousness.

THE E3 PERSONALITY TEST

PLEASE TAKE THE FOLLOWING PERSONALITY TEST
PRIOR TO READING FURTHER.
THIS WILL ENSURE A MORE ACCURATE TEST RESULT.

It is important to take this test with a mindset of being on a vacation or experiencing a neutral circumstance in your life because personality can shift depending on circumstances. Our personality may be different at work than when we are holding a baby in our arms. We are more directed in the first situation and more compassionate in the second. Situations trigger us to use different components of our personality. So as you take the test, think about being in a neutral place as you circle your answers.

The test has three sections with each section including two categories of ten statements. Though there are a total of sixty test statements, you will only circle thirty.

First, read the three or four sentences that best describes that category. Choose the category that best describes you. Then, for each of the ten statements, circle the one that pertains to you in a neutral situation. If both statements apply, choose the one that describes you the best. (That may mean 51% of the time.)

Later, you will go back and see the color that relates to that statement on the answer key. The answers will be denoted as R (Red), O (Orange), Y(Yellow) and G (Green). Tally up how many statements you circled for each of the color personalities. This reveals your personality ratio.

E3 Personality Test

I apply logic to solve most problems.

I am very detailed oriented and enjoy knowing the inner mechanism of things.

I am good at confronting people when something needs to be said.

If these statements characterize your personality, go to statements 1-10.

I apply understanding and consider all people's feelings to solve problems.

I am less detail oriented and prefer to work with things that are more artistic and creative than mechanical.

I prefer not to be confrontative. I am concerned with people's feelings.

I prefer to let things ride instead of a confrontation. Things usually work out fine.

If these statements characterize your personality, go to statements 11-20.

FOR EACH PAIR, CIRCLE THE STATEMENT THAT BEST DESCRIBES YOU IN A NEUTRAL SETTING.

1.
   a. I believe in traditional values and beliefs.
   b. I have my own unique values which often disagree with what others believe.

2.
   a. I typically pride myself on looking for new and better ways to do things.
   b. I typically will stick with a proven way of doing something.

3.
   a. I feel strength in working with a team of people and believe in the chain of command.
   b. I prefer working alone on projects without others around to complicate things.

4.
   a. I prefer assigned work to be outlined in detail including expectations and goals.
   b. I prefer assigned work to be detail-free allowing me to expand the project as I see fit.

5.
   a. I am theoretical.
   b. I am practical.

6.
   a. A good answer is better than a good question.
   b. A good question is better than a good answer.

7.
   a. My mind often thinks of alternative ways to reach the same goal.
   b. I keep my attention on what needs to be done to complete a task.

8.
   a. In problem solving, I am excited by pondering possibilities leading to new answers.
   b. In problem solving, it is easier to choose an accepted and proven method.

9.
   a. I consider myself and my thoughts to be mainstream.
   b. I find myself and my thoughts to be different and more complex than most others.

10.
   a. I need to concentrate on one thing at a time when completing a task.

b. I can have several things happening at once when I am completing a task.

FOR EACH PAIR, CIRCLE THE STATEMENT THAT BEST DESCRIBES YOU IN A NEUTRAL SETTING.

11.
   a. I enjoy the present and spend little time thinking about the future.
   b. I enjoy the present but find my thoughts drift to fun future plans and events.

12.
   a. I need to concentrate on one thing at a time when completing a task.
   b. I can have several things happening at once when I am completing a task.

13.
   a. I can get lost in rituals and become disconnected from the deeper meaning of an event.
   b. I feel ritual and ceremony connect me to the deeper meaning of an event.

14.
   a. I am theoretical.
   b. I am practical.

15.
   a. I believe in traditional values and beliefs.
   b. I have my own unique values which often disagree with what others believe.

16.
   a. In problem solving, it is easier to choose an accepted and proven method.
   b. In problem solving, I am excited by pondering possibilities leading to new answers.

17.
   a. I dislike doing things that are repetitious.
   b. I enjoy doing things that are repetitious.

18.

    a. I find myself and my thoughts to be different and more complex than most others.

    b. I consider myself and my thoughts to be mainstream.

19.

    a. A good answer is better than a good question.

    b. A good question is better than a good answer.

20.

    a. I take a conservative approach to most events.

    b. I like taking risks and I enjoy doing things differently.

SECTION II

I would categorize myself as traditional, preferring accepted and proven ways of doing things.

Following rules is an important part of what makes the world function properly.

I am OK with doing repetitive jobs with predictable outcomes.

If these statements characterize your personality, go to statements 21-30.

I would categorize myself as a freethinker or someone who thinks out-of-the-box.

I will follow rules that make sense to me, but the world is not black-and-white. Rules need to be constantly reevaluated and improved.

I prefer jobs involving new activities and constant challenges allowing me to problem solve.

If these statements characterize your personality, go to statements 31-40.

FOR EACH PAIR, CIRCLE THE STATEMENT THAT BEST DESCRIBES YOU IN A NEUTRAL SETTING.

21.
  a. I am willing to confront someone when the situation calls for it.
  b. I am less willing to confront someone. Things usually work themselves out.

22.
  a. I find solutions based on everyone's feelings and input work the best.
  b. I find that logical answers always give the best solutions.

23.
  a. I pride myself on being polite and kind.
  b. I pride myself on being respectful and honoring those that have earned it.

24.
  a. I believe productivity and the ability to work hard are important qualities.
  b. I believe being sensitive and understanding are important qualities.

25.
  a. I consider myself to be a logical person.
  b. I consider myself to be a feeling person.

26.
  a. I typically give more to others than they give to me.
  b. I help people if they earn it or deserve it. I don't believe in handouts.

27.
  a. I dislike conflict and look to resolve conflicts by finding common ground.
  b. I am OK with conflict and believe I can learn and grow stronger through conflicts.

28.
  a. I process feelings inside and do not like to expose my feelings.
  b. I process feelings deeply over time and find great relief in sharing with close friends.

29.

   a. In relationships, I show commitment by providing and protecting.

   b. In relationships, I show commitment by emotional support and comfort.

30.

   a. I would like to solve problems quickly but there are so many things to consider.

   b. I am able to solve problems quickly through fast actions.

FOR EACH PAIR, CIRCLE THE STATEMENT THAT BEST DESCRIBES YOU IN A NEUTRAL SETTING.

31.

   a. I enjoy brainstorming big ideas but prefer to give the mechanical issues to someone else.

   b. I enjoy brainstorming big ideas as well as knowing the mechanical issues of a problem.

32.

   a. I enjoy connecting to a lot of people and having a lot of friends.

   b. I don't need to connect to a lot of people and can function without a lot of friends around.

33.

   a. I have no problem confronting people and telling it like it is.

   b. I tend to avoid confrontation. It is hard to be negative.

34.

   a. I am more private than most people and work things out in my head.

   b. I am outgoing and often use others as sounding boards for my thoughts.

35.

   a. I believe in morals but dislike them when they are righteous, rigid or used to control.

   b. I define myself as having high morals and believe others should have them as well.

36.

   a. I see myself as an emotional being.

b. I am logical in nature and dislike emotions getting in the way.

37.

a. It is the nature of relationships to come and go.

b. When I lose a friend, it affects me more deeply than most people.

38.

a. It is not my problem when someone is depressed or in a mood. They will work it out.

b. I am compelled to help someone who is depressed.

39.

a. I find it difficult to outwardly express caring and loving feelings.

b. I find it hard sometimes to contain feelings and compassion for my family and friends.

40.

a. I believe being analytical and having skepticism is very important in life.

b. I feel good inside when I am connected and compassionate to others.

SECTION III

I am very passionate and active with groups and causes I believe in.

I tend to be outspoken and I enjoy meeting and interacting with new people.

I start projects quickly, believing that if problems arise, they can be worked out along the way. You won't get the job done if you spend too much time trying to figure things out ahead of time.

If these statements characterize your personality, go to statements 41-50.

I have beliefs but I don't need to share them with a lot of people.

I tend to sit back, watch, and learn about people before I interact with them.

I like to take my time when making decisions or when I get ready for an event.

I try to solve most problems before I start a project.

I really don't like things to go wrong with projects I have worked on.

If these statements characterize your personality, go to statements 51-60.

FOR EACH PAIR, CIRCLE THE STATEMENT THAT BEST DESCRIBES YOU IN A NEUTRAL SETTING.

41.
  a. I see myself as logical and practical.
  b. I see myself as theoretical and experimental.

42.
  a. I prefer work that involves brainstorming and expansion of ideas.
  b. I prefer work that highlights my productivity.

43.
  a. I believe there is more *out there* than what we can see or touch.
  b. I believe in things you can see and touch. Things are either real or not real.

44.
  a. Righteous moral standards cannot accommodate gray areas that exist in life.
  b. The world community lacks high moral standards.

45.
  a. The health of the planet and all living things is one of our most important issues.
  b. Environmentalism must balance the needs of industry and the needs of wildlife.

46.
  a. I see myself as a big thinker that loses interest in the details and mechanical issues.
  b. I pride myself on knowing the fine details and inner workings of a project.

47.

    a. I have my own unique values, despite what others think.

    b. I believe in traditional values.

48.

    a. In problem solving, I am excited by pondering possibilities leading to new answers.

    b. In problem solving, it is easier to choose an accepted and proven method.

49.

    a. A good question is better than a good answer.

    b. A good answer is better than a good question.

50.

    a. I believe the world needs a chain of command and levels of power based on merit and hard work. This keep order in our world.

    b. I believe in an egalitarian world where everyone is equal. Everyone has unique talents. The important part is recognizing and finding where our gifts work the best. If everyone were to do this, the world could reach its potential.

FOR EACH PAIR, CIRCLE THE STATEMENT THAT BEST DESCRIBES YOU IN A NEUTRAL SETTING.

51.

    a. In relationships, I show affection by giving emotional support and comfort.

    b. In relationships, I show affection by providing, protecting and problem solving.

52.

    a. I am creative and often have a sense what people will like and won't like.

    b. I am more logical in nature and I can figure out what people need or want.

53.

    a. I have my own unique values, despite what others think.

b. I believe in traditional values.

54.

    a. A good question is better than a good answer.

    b. A good answer is better than a good question.

55.

    a. I take a conservative approach to most events and use proven methods.

    b. I like taking risks and I enjoy doing things differently if it pushes me to a higher level.

56.

    a. I push myself by "raising the bar" on my activities, appreciating efficiency and accuracy.

    b. I enjoy creating with my hands. I don't have to push myself to enjoy what I am doing.

57.

    a. Usually, I can find all the information I need on my own, making fast logical decisions.

    b. I enjoy input from others, and it can take a while to find a solution I know is a good one.

58.

    a. I am OK with change in regular small amounts, as big changes sometime backfire.

    b. I am OK with big changes as it is exciting to see our ultimate potential.

59.

    a. I wish to be appreciated for my encouraging, nurturing skills.

    b. I desire to be competent, efficient and accomplished.

60.

    a. I enjoy multitasking and problem solving.

    b. I enjoy doing one thing at a time and I cherish time when I am not doing anything.

E3 PERSONALITY TEST ANSWERS

1AR	11AO	21AR	31AG	41AR	51AO
1BY	11BG	21BO	31BY	41BG	51BY
2AY	12AO	22AO	32AG	42AG	52AO
2BR	12BG	22BR	32BY	42BR	52BY
3AR	13AG	23AO	33AY	43AG	53AY
3BY	13BO	23BR	33BG	43BR	53BO
4AR	14AG	24AR	34AY	44AG	54AY
4BY	14BO	24BO	34BG	44BR	54BO
5AY	15AO	25AR	35AG	45AG	55AO
5BR	15BG	25BO	35BY	45BR	55BY
6AR	16AO	26AO	36AG	46AG	56AY
6BY	16BG	26BR	36BY	46BR	56BO

7AY	17AG	27AO	37AY	47AG	57AY
7BR	17BO	27BR	37BG	47BR	57BO
8AY	18AG	28AR	38AY	48AG	58AO
8BR	18BO	28BO	38BG	48BR	58BY
9AR	19AO	29AR	39AY	49AG	59AO
9BY	19BG	29BO	39BG	49BR	59BY
10AR	20AO	30AO	40AY	5OAR	60AY
10BY	20BG	30BR	40BG	50BG	60BO

R = RED O = ORANGE Y = YELLOW G = GREEN

Dr. William D. Mehring

THE FOUR BASIC PERSONALITY COLORS

Now let's take a look at the four basic colors of the personality that we each contain within us. Most of us use a main personality and then a secondary balancing personality. It is the unique combinations that give us our skills, attributes and our life lessons. The characteristics of each color as outlined in this chapter are indicative of the early stages of each personality. Before we go deeper into the personalities, I just want to point out that the personality looks different early on compared to how it looks when it gains life experiences. As we harmonize the dysfunctional parts of our personality that do not serve us, we look and act differently. Please keep in mind that we may have already done a lot of transformational work and that some of these characteristics might remind us of when we were younger. Who we are is constantly changing. It is important to note that the personality color descriptions are *general traits*. Individuals may fit the majority of a color description, rather than matching all of the criteria verbatim.

68

RED

Red is the most prevalent personality in the Western world. The Red personality perceives the world through the left hemisphere meaning they will see reality through the five senses of sight, smell, hearing, taste and touch. These senses are processed on the left side of the brain and within a logic-based system. The Red personality is characterized as traditional, structured, responsible, realistic, pragmatic, practical, family and detail oriented, dogmatic, down to earth, loyal, faith-based and hard-working. Reds are often followers of traditional power structure, following a chain of command and earning one's way to the top. Reds get things done. They are up front, clear with their thoughts and not afraid of confrontation so one always knows where one stands with the Red person. They enjoy competitions, sports, races and witnessing personal triumph through physical and mental determination. Reds are also usually the first people to pitch in and help when needed. They enjoy a very tight family structure and are dutifully bound and are good at making friends and alliances. They are great providers and protectors for family. Reds reach out to the less fortunate with a helping hand. The Red personality embodies the positive archetypes of Warrior, Protector and Leader. Their negative archetype is the Victim.

Red personalities value work and enjoy work that is challenging, structured, and complex. Many are CEO's and business owners. Reds are in finance, real estate, sports, construction, factory work, and law enforcement. They are religious leaders, lawyers, historians, doctors and politicians. They often start clubs and institutions and enjoy everyone sharing a mutual goal or a mission statement but if the Red personality has not harmonized his/her issues, the club could be focused on perpetuating a specific or rigid ideology.

What are the life lessons that transform and balance the Red personality? Generally, Reds transform when they see someone get hurt as a result of specific actions, whether their own actions or others'. This is driven by a deep sense of fairness. Early on in the Red struggle, the parameters of fairness and right and wrong will be manipulated for the need to win. Remember that the left brain has an urgent need to survive, as well as being home base for the ego. As a result, sometimes Reds do what is necessary to be triumphant. As with all colors, balance can be found by integrating what they lack. For the Red, this means they can find balance by spending more time on the right side of the brain. This means coming to peace with or embodying more of the belief syste ms of the right brained personality.

Red is the most common personality in the United States. The Red person is very capable of speaking their truth and tends to be confrontational with a strong need to be in control. Our societal structure and laws have always been influenced by the Red personality. The un harmonized Red resonates with laws based on the biblical concept on 'an eye for an eye' seeing right and wrong in black and white terms. How one perceives right and wrong and subsequent actions depends more on the personality or perspective than reality or truth. The un- harmonized Red sets up rules that may be rigid, limiting and easily manipulated to serve the needs and causes of the Red personality. But as with all personalities, as they journey through life, Reds become more pliable, less survival based and more empathetic. A Red personality can change quickly when they witness the suffering and pain of others. One good example is a Red who is a bad loser early on in life but matures into a good sportsman, still preferring to win, but not requiring it. A Red often chases the feeling of worthiness. This leads to a need for power, control, domination over the enemy, loyalty and uniformity.

The Red has a dominant need for a strong family unit that will always be there for support, a need for money, power, control and to be on top. Reds want to earn their way to the top to feel honored and respected. All this really boils down to being a part of their group and to be important. Family is very important group followed by membership in organizations with people of shared "traditional values".

However, we attract what we fear. Reds need to confront and be okay with who they are without power, wealth and control. If not, the universe will present difficult lessons that are imperative for their growth and long term happiness. For example, the un-harmonized, wealthy Red personality who has acquired the "trophy wife" will in all probability lose half of his wealth, his company, and control over people. The pro football player, who believes he is superior due to his physicality, status, power and money, may be headed for a physical injury that crushes his ego-driven world. Many people are ego-based, hence fear-based. These scenarios are prevalent throughout our culture.

The correlations between the ego chasing and those who lose what they have chased are very high. It is why most millionaires have been bankrupt so many times. Donald Trump has filed bankruptcy four times. The highs and lows are a powerful lesson teaching acceptance of who we are, regardless of money or status. The pro football player doesn't need to quit playing football. He needs to stop using the game to feel more worthy than others. If Reds feel better about themselves when they are in a bigger house, driving a fancier car, or are able to convert more people to their ideology, their consequence will be more life lessons. This consequence is the soul working overtime to create opportunities for transformation, not punishment. All people and all personalities are ego driven, but the Red personality has much more work to do in the material/physical world than the others personality types because this is how they measure themselves more than the other personalities. The lesson of 'attracting what you fear' is one that is ultimately taught to all personalities.

Another common theme for the Red personality is a dislike for weakness. This theme correlates to the desire for power, domination, uniformity, and the creation of a chain of command. We see many instances of this in movies and popular culture. <u>A Few Good Men</u> is a perfect example. In this movie, two men are being charged in the death of a fellow soldier. They had committed a code *Red* (a euphemism for a violent extrajudicial punishment) on a fellow soldier displaying nonconformity and weakness. The soldier died as a result. The film is filled with Red personalities. There is the archetypal Warrior portrayed very well by Jack Nicholson. His character was consumed with ideologies of good and evil and the protection of the boundaries and institution of the United States. Every military action was justified in order to dominate the foe. He represents hierarchy, a chain of command, a uniformity of beliefs and had no problem twisting the truth or pulling strings with the many loyal liaisons he made to win his cause. The character clearly demonstrates the manipulating of what is right and wrong to justify a closely held rigid belief system. This character illustrates the Red personality early on in the process of harmonization and balance.

The protagonist in <u>A Few Good Men</u> is a good example of how the Red personality can evolve. The soldier realized the error in his belief system about weakness. He went from thinking that the way to deal with weakness was to beat someone down to make them stronger, to realizing the need to protect and understand those who are more vulnerable and even help them find their strengths. By the end of the film, the young Marine transforms. His internal moral compass guides him to know that he can no longer stand by and watch the downtrodden continue to be harmed. He can no longer obey orders that are wrong just because they are orders from a higher up. He embodies the archetype of Protector and this is what makes the Red personality heroic. They have the ability to stand up to authority and society's pressures because they do not conform when they know the action is unjust or wrong.

The harmonized Red personality represents our world's greatest heroes with the core of a protector and someone who strives for noble beliefs such as justice, fairness and freedom, without manipulation. They are kind and thoughtful without reservation or an agenda of assimilation and reach out to help the less fortunate. They are great teachers of inner strength and perseverance. Un-harmonized Reds want to teach, but their method is to use fear and ridicule. This is seen in many sports coaches. The more harmonized Reds become, the more they teach using encouragement and empowerment.

This same theme is revealed in a movie titled <u>Radio</u> where the high school football coach discovered his Red football players beating up on a mentally disabled student, named Radio. As the coach (also a Red personality) began to protect this young man from the taunting and abuse of the other players, the coach saw the unique individual the disabled student was. Another hallmark of the harmonized Red is a deep sense of fairness, equality and acceptance of differences. The coach developed great compassion for this student who was different and who had unique gifts. At one point in the movie, students and parents and townspeople were against the coach's connection to Radio. It took the commitment and resolve of his Red energy to persevere through the pressures of the whole community. Again, doing what's right and not conforming is evidence of a harmonized Red personality.

The un-evolved and un-harmonized Red personality commonly involves greed and intolerant ideologies. It is sometimes difficult to differentiate between evolved and un-evolved Reds because they both use ideologies such as freedom. One uses ideologies to hide their fear-based and self-serving actions and the other does it because it feels right, as well as to serve others. Every personality has its lessons to ultimately harmonize their belief systems. As long as our greatest thought form is fear, we will keep attracting the lessons that will show us we need *not* fear. The following list will assist in creating new actions that will harmonize the Red belief systems. Remember the guideline is to do the opposite action that was done in the past.This will harmonize the belief system that wants to be changed.

- Realize that things are not black or white. Reds need awareness about how they categorize everything into good and bad, life or death, and friend and foe. This is a part of the survival mechanism that exists within the individualistic and separate view of the left brain. This survival instinct influences many decisions of the Red. Life is more about gray than it is black-and-white and the Red personality may want to explore not making *foes* out of those they do not understand. This is especially important in religion.
- Begin seeing the world as interconnected with humanity a part of one big family. Other people, ethnicities, and religions are not necessarily out to cause harm. Step out of the box and learn about other traditions. Examine resistance to the fact that others have valid opinions and beliefs. Help those in need. Use strength to help people find their own gifts.
- Realize that life is not tidy or uniform. It is messy and diverse.
- Be aware of comparing yourself to others. Work on letting go of the ego's need to compare, judge and put other people down.
- Open up.

All of these harmonizing actions will result in fewer hardships on the body as constant battle creates an energetic drain that leads to all sorts of negative beliefs and actions. Doing this work will lead to less rigidity, humility, generosity and an ability to help the world to be a better and safer place.

ORANGE

Orange personalities are some of the nicest, most thoughtful people you'll ever meet. People with the orange personality initially perceive through the five senses, including seeing their world in a more literal, concrete sense. They are comfortable with traditional values and roles and are very sensitive to what other people think. Although one would think the Orange is intuitive, they are masters at understanding nonverbal communication. They have studied and correlated the nonverbal clues of what others are truly thinking. They have also put a lot of energy into anticipating the needs of others. As their life experience expands, they integrate more of their intuition which is focused on the thoughts and wishes of those around them, and whether the person is someone to be feared or not. They are really good at picking up vibes.

Oranges process information through the right side of the brain, which sees things through a feeling-based reality. Because they perceive through the five senses, this means that perceptions and processing are occurring on both sides of the brain. Oranges perceive with the left brain (the physical world) and process through the right (universal concepts) so the neuro-synaptic information must pass through the corpus callosum to the opposite side of the brain. This crossing from one side to another is unique. The two hemispheres of the brain almost need a program to translate information perceived on one side and processed on the other. It's like a Mac talking to a PC. Two worlds coming together in one personality can create a little more confusion than the Red or Green personalities, which stay lateralized. This sets up a little bit more conflict within the Orange personality which can result in more lessons and greater potential for change.

The Orange is a very empathetic personality. Oranges wish to be accepted and appreciated by everyone they meet making them people pleasers and peacekeepers. Orange women and many of the men are very good at creating calm, soothing places where everyone can relax. Oranges know how to comfort those around them and have great capacity to feel the pain that others feel. Because of this, Oranges can have some sadness about how the world is so hurtful. It is not unusual for them to gravitate towards dramatic themes in books and movies that show the hardships that people endure. They continually wish for a kinder, more considerate world and have a constant state of internal worry. They may deny that it's there because being wrong or being criticized is very upsetting, but they often say, "I worry about this and I worry about that." Oranges are socially responsible, follow the majority, and like things to be peaceful. They are always asking for permission and want others to do the same. They are great caretakers because they are polite, courageous, and generous, and tremendously loyal.

Oranges are very private and don't like to expose their weaknesses as they want so much to be accepted by everyone. They send their extreme benevolence into the world in the hopes that it will be returned, but this does not always happen. The positive archetype of Orange is the Caretaker. The flip side is that they can easily shift into the negative archetype Martry. A martyr is someone who tells the world that they have sacrificed themselves for others and received nothing in return, which is perfect for Oranges because they strive for praise and allegiance from others.

Oranges, like all the others, have certain abilities and tools, one being their profound enjoyment of beauty that includes everything from art, music, and nature to the laughter of a child. They are sensitive to emotional needs of others and are able to use color, music, and art to soothe or create any desired effect. It is acceptable to have repetition in their jobs because they can do the same task over and over. While Oranges can expand and receive more enjoyment out of a wonderful experience than most, they can also have a greater experience of suffering because they have difficulty experiencing life in a free flowing way due to worry.

Given all of these abilities and dispositions, Oranges commonly find jobs where they help and comfort people. They become great musicians, social workers, psychologists, child advocates, nurses, physical therapists, dental hygienists, food servers, receptionists, airline attendants, and executive assistants. Oranges also make great interior designers, artists, singers, painters, thespians, graphic designers. Another place they shine is working with animals and children because young children are rarely judgmental; children and pets are good for the Orange. They tend not to choose occupations of the greatest responsibility or where they must make many decisions that affect other people.

The Orange spends a lot of time seeking approval and help in reaching decisions. They gather opinions from lots of people and often will agree with the popular view even if it goes against their own. But when an Orange learns to hold their own, without bending to the whim of every new belief, they can rise to new heights. Oranges make great mediators and are capable of compromise. Oranges want everyone to be happy or at least mostly happy, and they bring people together and find common ground.

Oranges do have difficulty making quick decisions and they often feel the world is moving too fast. They do not process information quickly because they have to make sure that everyone's needs are met, that everything is perfect, that they will not be criticized or judged. Unfortunately, this is just not how life works and expecting things to go smoothly is unrealistic. For someone who is a worrier, every life event carries the potential for something to go wrong. The Orange personality will avoid involvement in projects that have an unknown outcome. Therefore, the Orange might be seen as a procrastinator, even a naysayer. Suggest a project and an orange will come up with many reasons why it will not work or should not be done. They also might just agree but never complete the task. Self-initiation is difficult so Oranges work best in groups with shared responsibility. Community is where oranges thrive and work brilliantly though they do struggle to speak up wishing that others could anticipate their needs so they don't have to ask. This seems perfectly reasonable to them as Oranges can anticipate the needs of others.

The Orange extrovert is outgoing, charismatic, and a group leader. The Orange introvert is a follower, good observer, quiet and thoughtful. Perhaps this is why they have such difficulty with people who are judgmental and critical. They do not like to go against the grain or the majority belief. They can become over stimulated by too much input. They dislike the feeling of being inadequate around quick decision-makers that surround them. This personality is the most sensitive and empathic of all of the personalities and has the ability to appreciate artwork, handicrafts, colors, music, singing, clouds across the sky and the glow of the sunset.

Oranges are genuinely liked by others because they are considerate, humble and strive to do the right thing for the common good. Politics is a good arena for the orange personality to learn how to confront opposition and move forward with what they feel is best. They wrestle with pleasing everyone while pushing forward and they want to reach across the aisle to unite the country. They usually have a history of being able to find solutions that work for various divergent views, that is, of course, if both parties have a desire to work things out. Knowing this about oranges helps us understand the internal conflict of President Barack Obama, who is an Orange personality in my opinion. The presidential experience will create many opportunities for President Obama to be okay with confrontation, as well as give him the ability to fight for what he believes in, instead of always looking for a consensus. Many of our presidents, both Republican and Democrat, have had some aspect of the Orange personality because voters value and this empathetic kindness in their leaders.

Orange people make very caring parents. All of the kids on the block want to visit the Orange mother's house; she will be the one making cookies and making sure everyone's well taken care of. If the man is the Orange personality, it is not unusual for him to marry a woman who is the leader of the family so he can be the nurturer. Because of their peacekeeper tendency, Orange parents can be soft, even wishy-washy, often not drawing a firm line until they become very angry. The Orange will give so much that they can give *too* much. Orange personalities create homes that are calm and comfortable with colors, crafts, flowers, art and music that invite others to stay a while.

There are issues that cause the Orange personality stress and chaos. They are constantly searching for acceptance and appreciation from others to feel validated. Being okay when others don't like them is a big lesson. The Orange defaults to putting other people's needs ahead of their own and they pride themselves on sensing what people need, how to make others comfortable, and tireless caretaking. None of the other personalities have the capacity to over give like an Orange. In their constant quest for acceptance, compromise and consensus, their own goals become less important. They often lose sight of their life's work and because they have lost themselves in over giving or pleasing other people. Finding out who they are, what they want to be, and expressing their needs and opinions is their greatest work. Oranges must also realize that their caretaking serves theri own need to be accepted and liked. Once this awareness occurs, the Orange is less likely to assume the role of the martyr.

When something goes wrong for the Orange, they assume they are to blame. They judge themselves and feel embarrassed for their actions. This self-deprecation constantly depletes their power to stand up for themselves and speak their truth. The Orange has an infinite capacity to worry when they are stressed, coming up with real and many more unreal fears that inhibit their growth. Many Oranges push through this fear of criticism and make themselves get things done, while others never allow themselves to get in this position. Oranges who resonate with the negative archetypes of Martyr and Victim strategize in two ways. They sabotage themselves by inventing reasons to avoid projects where they are either being forced to do something or where they may be a target for criticism.

The second strategy is escapism and blaming. Remember that Oranges avoid criticism at all costs so they blame others to defend their innocence. Oranges who have not harmonized their path need to escape to a safe place either their home, or a room in the home, where they can avoid people. The safe nest is the place to recover from over giving. The Orange tends to give so much that there is nothing left. This is why many Oranges prefer to stay home, and will find work that allows this. Orange men commonly become stay-at-home fathers or create a home business. However, if their fears overtake their life, the nest can turn into a cave because Oranges can hide in the dark. If the Oranges do not voice their needs, opinions or desires, they often use drugs and alcohol to escape, self-medicating as the doorway to the cave. Oranges are well practiced in creating a façade so they mask the use of drugs or other bad habits very well.

When I've spoken with my Orange patients about their dark habits, they tell me they are tired of being goody two-shoes, being perfect for society. The Orange feels controlled so they push back. There is a Taoist expression which states, "The more laws there are, the more people will want to break the laws." So there is either too much control which causes an overreaction of no self control. The Orange feels controlled by societal norms and expectations so they take on habits that society disapproves of. Closet activity may include eating, drinking, smoking, gambling, drugs, porn or other sexual addictions. However, the other possibility is that when the Orange personality feels controlled, instead of becoming a Martyr or a Victim, they can take the opportunity to stand up for themselves.

In relationships, the more the Orange gives, the more they are rewarded with acceptance and or praise. This can lead to over giving, a habitual chasing that gets stronger and results in a loss of identity. Their whole day is consumed with meeting the needs of others. Layered on this is the ability to be nice and kind and to be rewarded for this behavior. Oranges put on a happy face, even when they don't feel happy or fulfilled. They don't want to upset people or expose their insecurities to others or to themselves. So they adopt a mechanism of grinning and bearing it early on. Soon, they spend their days asking, "What can I do for you and how would you like me to look? Hello, nice to meet you, how would you like me to act? What can I do for you? May I help you? Can I assist you? Who can I be for you? How would you like me to change?"

Oranges mold themselves into what other people want exchanging their power for acceptance. They even surrender power trying to be a better giver than the next person. Oranges get lost in constantly morphing themselves for others and they struggle to sustain who they are in the face of becoming what other people want. Oranges allow the needs of others to take precedent over expressing their own needs or boundaries. It's impossible to make a boundary decision when Oranges don't know who they are or what they want. They are so worried about what other people feel and think that they can't form an opinion.

Oranges usually choose partners who are strong-willed and able to handle confrontation. This provides a knight in shining armor who will champion their opinions and do their bidding without them having to speak. They never have to take the hit as the front man and they have a strong protector. The downside is that these controlling partners can be physically and verbally abusive. As Oranges find their voice and independence, their strong-willed partners want to continue to be in charge making decisions and being the spokesperson. It is not uncommon for them to put down and belittle the Orange in the attempt to control them. This can be a great opportunity for change and growth. If Oranges need self-sufficiency, they will choose a Yellow partner. If they need passion and the ability to love, they will choose Green. If they need to learn strength and fortitude, they will pick a Red partner. All of these partners are teachers, as well as the Orange being their partner's teacher. The Orange in relationship demonstrates empathy, consideration, appreciation, politeness, and most importantly, that egotism is unacceptable.

Even though the situation is difficult, it is the perfect place for the Orange to speak their truth, create boundaries and be concerned with self-care. There will be a multitude of chances in the Orange person's life to find balance in the amount of giving they do as well as speaking their truth and being who they are. Romantic relationships are the opportunity Oranges need to practice all of the aspects of self- acceptance.

This brings us to a phenomenon I call "cut-and-chop." This phenomenon occurs when a person completely ignores, avoids or dispenses with somebody in their life. Typically the Orange personality makes a promise they really don't want to keep or they may have agreed to something to reduce conflict or to be nice. Oranges can also procrastinate on a task to the point where they are embarrassed to follow through. Since Oranges worry they will be blamed and criticized for their shortcomings and insecurities, they just permanently avoid the person or the situation rather than confront their feelings of inadequacy. This is "cut and chop." The ego avoids due to embarrassment or any other negative feelings which may have started small, but grew larger and larger over time making it impossible for the Orange to engage.

By now we understand that the Orange gives and gives and gives in relationship but feels nothing in return. Unfortunately, they do not express their needs hoping that their partner will just know what they need. This all leads to growing resentment and lack of connection with their partner. The partner interprets this behavior as moodiness and separation. The moods and separation will intensify until the partner asks what is wrong. The only other alternative is for the Orange personality to learn to ask for what they need.

In order to grow and change, the Orange must first identify and understand the issues that need to be transformed. Then, as long as they are not in any danger, they need to stay with the situations that trigger avoidance, isolation, martyrdom or resentment. The Orange needs to stay and face the issue so that they can choose a new path. Remember the process of the Evolution Cycle: awakening, self-remembrance, awareness, transition, transformation and transmutation. In a nutshell, the Orange must perceive and respond to the trigger situation differently. *Pushing* through the experience and making a different choice changes everything.

The Orange must become a doer saying 'yes' to life and using 'no' to set boundaries. Fear is always bigger than the reality and situations are temporary. Adapting and evolving through trigger experiences allows a more empowered person. Life is long and there is plenty of time to transform patterns set since childhood and make the soul changes needed.

Oranges need to make waves, express their needs and their opinions. This practice is vital. The method and delivery of that expression may be a little spicy at first, but that's okay. There may be righteous energy put forth to overcome shame, blame or guilt while they learn that speaking their truth is okay. Eventually, Oranges will discover that they can eliminate such feelings from their internal vocabulary altogether and express, express, express without looking back. Self-expression is so empowering that the self-deprecation and negative mind talk will stop and Oranges can become more self aware in a positive way. Allowing others to take the reins of giving will also improve relationships.

Another big task for Oranges is to examine why they worry and work to shatter that model. There is a fear of not measuring up, being found out, and not being the expert that they are supposed to be. The Orange wrestles with the internal fear of being wrong or not good enough which invades all aspects of their life. The Orange must learn to be themselves, even if that self is grumpy and contrary.

It is also essential for Oranges who are creative by nature, to become invigorated by their own creativity. It could be singing, painting, needlepoint, wood carving, cooking, or photography. Creativity will increase joy. A good practice is to embrace a finished project even when it is not perfect. Oranges need to learn to be easier on themselves because they *are* good enough. Meditation is also an important regenerative tool to give time and space for the inward journey.

The big journey for the Orange personality is self acceptance; to be okay without approval from others. Situations where they experience rejection will provide opportunity to hear criticism objectively, and receive it without being defensive or becoming self deprecating. They must resist over giving, enabling, and caretaking; and the Orange must put themselves first. I must reiterate that Oranges must strive to get out there and act, be risqué, and make some waves instead of hiding in a cave. Historian Laurel Thatcher Ulrich said, "Well-behaved women seldom make history." I love this quote because if you substitute "women" with "Orange", it is a great motto. Well-behaved Oranges seldom make history. The Orange personality can feel more alive, directed, refreshed, on track, internally connected, and happy. These are the rewards of harmonizing.

YELLOW

The Yellow personality perceives through the physical and the energetic worlds. But perception through the five senses and the intuition creates some internal conflict. I have talked about the traditional, black-and-white, literal, and solitary survival based view of the world that comes from perceiving by the left brain. I also introduced the connected, infinite, free and harmonious view of the world when perceived through the right brain. The Yellow personality has to juggle these two opposing perceptions.

There are several ways in which the Yellow can deal with this. Early in the Yellow's life, they typically prioritize the physical world because they generally process through the logical left side of their brain. This Yellow individual will be more traditional, dualistic and literal, but at the same time very spiritual. Because Yellows perceive through the right brain as well, they don't buy into the archetype of Creator as a white-haired man on Mount Olympus who punishes those who are not obedient. The right brain views the Divine as an energetic formless being that is beyond comprehension. Right brained thinkers believe that everything, living and inanimate is part of this consciousness. George Lucas, the writer and director of the Star Wars series, summed it up the best when he articulated the concept of "The Force." If Yellows perceive on the right side of the brain, they see themselves and everything in harmony communicating with this universal consciousness. This personality embodies big thinkers who seem well beyond their years. This personality accounts for a small amount of the population at large but makes up a large percentage of innovators in the fields of philosophy and social change.

When the Yellow personality is young, they can develop a very tender underbelly. As they age, they develop a hard logical outer shell. The longer they develop this shell, the better the Yellow becomes at hiding their inner softness. Yellows can lack emotions. They are born processing through logic and the longer they do this, the longer they perceive through the five senses. As they grow older, the Yellow personality discovers that all of life's ups and downs cannot be navigated by reason alone. This is when they begin to integrate the right side of the brain. Yellows will use more intuition and process information through feelings. This integration can be a difficult phase of the Yellow journey as they begin to perceive and process with both sides of the brain. It is like the transformation of a robot into an artist. Two characters from the movies embody the Yellow personality. Spock, the Vulcan from the original Star Trek, represents this transformation. Vulcans model the Yellow personality believing everything can be solved by the discipline of logic and mind control. But even the Vulcan learns he must expand into the world of feeling.

The core of the Yellow personality is efficiency. It is no surprise this personality yields great inventors, always discovering innovative ways of doing things. Enjoyment comes from thinking, problem solving, and pondering the big questions. Yellows can be extroverted or introverted, are decidedly independent, headstrong, and are both logical and creative in their problem solving. They are self-initiating, self-respecting, self-motivating, and self-reliant. The Yellow person is very ambitious and completion oriented making them responsible providers for the family. They have a very high moral compass, and can be judgmental and questioning of authority. All of this can lead to rigid belief systems.

Yellows are born micromanagers because they want others to be as competent and as efficient as they are. They will search out every permutation to the outcome of a problem before they give you the right way to do it. The right-brained perceiving Yellow enjoys finding multiple approaches to solving problems as well as having an amazing ability to manifest outcomes using both the energetic and physical world. They love information and know how all systems work; from financial institutions to combustion engines. Yellow personalities are never satisfied in their pursuit of being good enough. They strive to be better and better and better constantly pushing the bar higher. They have organized the best way to complete daily routines and happily teach others their methods.

Yellows exhibit perfectionism perhaps so they can be the ultimate authority. They must truly live their beliefs so they can maintain this level of superiority. If they do not, then someone might point out their hypocrisy, which removes them from the position of judge. The Yellow personality is typically polite, yet skeptical and sometimes even cynical. They share the Orange's propensity for the 'cut-and-chop' strategy but in the case of the Yellow, they use the method to punish the banished person rather than as a mechanism to avoid their own shortcomings. Yellows use the 'cut and chop' method because someone goes against the moral compass or insinuates that the Yellow made mistakes.

Yellows like independence partly so that they do not have to rely on a world that commonly makes mistakes. This allows them to avoid their feelings of betrayal and disappointment. They crave and insist upon the freedom to explore their thoughts about the world. They enjoy testing their own proficiency and overcoming obstacles making problem solving a common pastime. Yellows have difficulty with people who are inefficient, ignorant, over-emotional and dramatic personalities. For the Yellow, these traits lead to failure. They become very upset with people who try to limit their expansive thinking or social freedoms.

All of these likes and dislikes make the Yellow discover new and better ways for doing things whether it be how to design a better mousetrap or how to evoke greater sociological and personal change. They are a wealth of information, enjoy fixing things, are technology wizards and are outstanding at <u>Jeopardy</u>. They are logical with a side order of feelings which allows them to find solutions that few others could. They can also render decisions of great moral debate easily. Everything they do will be done quickly and thoroughly.

These traits make Yellows have high aptitudes for math, engineering, physics, design, invention, politics, law, and social change. Many theologians, particularly rabbis, are Yellow personalities because rabbis love to wrestle with multidimensional concepts that push them to find the deeper meanings and answers within. The same is true of academics. The Yellow personality also prefers individual athletics to team sports and like to conquer running then cycling, then swimming. Thus the Yellow is ideally suited to the triathlon as this sport takes great mental and physical perseverance.

In my opinion, famous Yellow personalities include Gandhi, Robert F. Kennedy, Hilary Clinton, Stephen Hawking and the Dalai Lama. Martin Luther King, Jr., and Mother Teresa are most likely a combination of yellow and green. The addition of Green increases the passionate wish for peace. Green is the color we explore in the next chapter.

The positive Yellow archetypes are Provider, Teacher, Philosopher, Revolutionary, and Leader. The negative archetypes include the Student, Silent Child, and even Sadist. The dark side of Yellow is ego chasing not just to micromanage others but to manipulate them. This manipulation is how the Yellow feels powerful. If a Yellow person has internal tension and stress they often feel soothed by creating tension in others. They will manipulate them into believing things that are not true just to see others in chaos. The Yellow ego chases acknowledgment, appreciation, love and loyalty from a very select few. They look for this acknowledgment through efficiency and achievement and pride themselves on the ability to solve any problem. They are always trying to attain superiority in the world of hierarchy, but thrive in the world of intellectual pursuits. They also pride themselves on their high level of morality, relishing playing both the judge and the jury. They strive to be self-sufficient and look for ways to congratulate themselves instead of relying on others. They are the true multitask people, creating new ways to do things, get them done right and get them done on time. In a nutshell, Yellows like being productive with a sense of purpose. The purpose cannot be small; it must be grand and contribute to a greater good.

The Yellow ego chasing is to overcome the fear of failure or not being good enough. It is for this reason that the Yellow continuously confronts new challenges, constantly pushing to the point where they might fail. This is what humans do. We create situations so we can confront our greatest fear: accepting ourselves as we are. Yellows raise the competitive bar so high, that it inevitably leads to failure. Yellows tire from trying to control the many parameters of their life. They become exhausted from proving they are superior, right, and moral. The Yellow personality's great moment is when there is self-acceptance.

Yellows need to stop the chasing and discover the power of the present and the process rather than the outcome of task completion. This is very difficult because the Yellow personality is turned on by multitasking and efficiently getting things done. Imagine the Yellow writing a "To Do" list. The many circuits of Yellow's mind begin tracking, managing and routing efficiency into every stroke of completing the list. The lengthy list seems impossible but one after another items are checked off, making them feel very powerful in their efficiency. Adrenaline surges as they shift into the realm of high performance. At the end of the day, they check the last thing off the list, finishing the impossible and feeling accomplished and proud.

The next day, the Yellow hungers for a new list to conquer. Day after day this goes on with the list growing to make it more challenging. Over-achieving for a few days may be necessary now and then, however, this ego chasing is a daily occurrence for the Yellow personality. Yellows live for the future and never enjoy the moment and when the body keeps this pace without rest, the cost is severe. They are running on the multitasking track and cannot get off. When they do not get everything on the list checked off, they are very disappointed in themselves. This causes their body to feel tired and drained while their mind loses its plasticity from the overuse of efficient thinking tracks. Repetitive behaviors age the brain; new thoughts and experiences keep the body and the brain young. Appreciating art, sculpting with clay, learning new languages, and mining the depth of poetry and great writing, as well as exploring, are all ways of defying the effects of aging. It is very challenging for a Yellow not to be productive because they love creating things, rather than creating new experiences. Yellows even produce during vacation rather than simply relaxing. The yellow's idea of a vacation includes mountain climbing, visiting educational landmarks, or building a Habitat for Humanity project.

Yellows maintain very high moral standards for their actions, and insist that those close to them possess these standards as well. This puts the Yellow in position of judge and people who don't have these moral standards and intellect are not invited to be their friends. An opposite action is for Yellows to gain awareness when they judge others. Judging happens during the ego's game of comparison and hierarchy. To Yellow personalities, there is nothing better than being the judge: the ultimate ruling position.

Actions that integrate the right brain function can be transforming for the Yellow. These include creative expression such as photography and painting. The Yellow personality is suited to photography because of its technical aspects. Anything that excites the artistic and creative mind is great work for the Yellow personality as this forms a connection to inner knowledge and wisdom.

Meditation is wonderful for the Yellow for a number of reasons. It is a solitary pursuit so there is no judgment or hierarchy. It challenges the Yellow to participate in an activity that while outwardly seeming non productive, inwardly mediation increases mental plasticity as well as increasing cellular rejuvenation to the frontal lobes of the brain. Meditation also increases circulation as well as increasing the brain's mental and spiritual capacities. Meditation is a way to connect to the energetic world beyond the five senses and once the Yellow develops the intuitive skill set, watch out world! They become avid and disciplined meditation practitioners realizing the potential of using the whole brain.

The most demanding and important step for most Yellows is to become emotionally vulnerable. Typically Yellows express their love through being providers and supporters of others' personal growth. This is not enough. For the Yellow to access their whole brain, they must engage in the world of feelings, exposing that tender underbelly of emotions. Learning how to touch and be touched, learning how to give and receive tender love, learning how to express emotions without control is the most efficient and logical way to become feeling. The result of this integration is where Yellows experience their greatest unfolding.

GREEN

The Green personality perceives through the right brain. All consciousness circulates freely, which is why the Green personality is very intuitive. Greens usually lose some of this ability around adolescence when they become absorbed in what others think of them but in time, Greens return to their original feeling of connection. To be fully intuitive and connected, the Green personality must actively resolve their stress inducing emotional dynamics.

Greens connect themselves to all things making them great advocates for human and animal rights, as well environmental causes. These Greens are tree huggers. Since they perceive a vast and endless world, they want to mirror this vastness in their physical world. Hence, they prefer openness and freedom to tight closed spaces. They do not like being held down or told what to think . Because the right brain senses many things at once greens have several projects happening at the same time.

Greens process on the right side of the brain, in the world of the emotions. This world of feelings comes with great surges of powerful neurochemicals. These neurochemicals evoke the urges which compel or motivate greens to do things not considered in the logical world. No one drives all night to get paperwork from the office, but most greens have driven all night to see their first love.

Greens are outspoken, charismatic, flexible, gregarious, passionate, robust, multitasking and exciting. They avoid conflict, and are exuberant, theoretical, tender, loving, imaginative, creative, empathic, and have profound intuitive and healing abilities. To many people, Greens look a little spacey and speak random thoughts, or forget what they're saying in the middle of a sentence. They are also forgetful in general. The Green personality has a sense of immediacy which leads to impatience.

The Green wants to be connected and they will search for and study ways to make that happen with others and with themselves. They spend most of their life reaching out to others but at some point they need to turn inward. This is when the Green finds the connection to their inner wisdom and this helps with the issues resulting from feeling disconnected. These include loss, grief and abandonment. As Greens seek to be in connection with all things, they often experience great feelings of loss when something or someone dies.

Greens dislike loneliness, repetition, boredom, being controlled and not being loved. Greens are freethinkers embodying the positive archetypes of Lover, Healer, Activist and in some cases, Revolutionary. The negative archetype is Narcissist. A disconnected Green can quickly spiral into deep despair and hopelessness.

Greens have the ability to awaken passion in others. They are capable of creating excitement so they make great leaders and teachers. As theoretical thinkers, they make great leaps in their knowledge and understanding seeing humanity's infinite possibilities. Where others dwell on the obstacles, the nature of the Green personality is thinking about the possibilities. Greens are great salespeople because they sell their enthusiasm for the product.

Greens morph into different personalities for love and connection. Because of this ability to change into Red, Orange, or Yellow, Greens are personality chameleons. It is sometimes not easy to identify a Green because their core personality may be varied and fluid. Again, this adaptability is due to flexibility and longing for connection.

Green's abilities include healing, leadership, networking, insight and seeing the big picture. They use these abilities in career and relationships. But when a Green over gives or panders, this is a sign they are chasing the ego's needs. One example is a Green healer's tendency to be "Super Doctor." Super Doctor wants to heal the patient faster than normal, want the patient to appreciate them more, and wants to become their friend. Super Doctors don't bill for extra treatment time and give away free medicine. This is a good example of being motivated by longing for connection. In fact, Greens need to be super at everything they do so others will want to be with them. If their motivation for this behavior originates in feeling not good enough, it is ego chasing. But if the behavior is motivated by the authentic self truly wanting to improve, the ego is not at work.

There is a lot of ego chasing on the part of the Greens in relationships as they are prone to over giving. They often act as peacemakers in their attempt to stay connected and keep relationships strong. This can easily turn into the Green becoming a victim of abuse because Greens fantasize about the relationships and deny when things are really bad. Greens are shocked when partnerships crumble because they do not anticipate the end. The best way to combat this is for Green to cultivate the ability to be alone. Developing an internal awareness and connection will assist

Greens in knowing they do not need relationships to feel content. Solo time also helps Greens with abandonment, which is their biggest issue. Many Green personalities suffer a significant loss early in their life. It might be the loss of a parent through death or divorce or the loss of a sibling, best friend or other close relationship. Most Green personalities have first hand knowledge of being deserted.

When it comes to a romantic relationship, the Green needs intensity and excitement. Unfortunately, it is unusual for one Green to attract another because they share too many of the same negative issues: stubbornness, narcissism and neediness. They choose partners who do not share their language and end up disappointed with the lack of depth and intensity in the relationship. Once the Green personalities have harmonized their negative issues, two Greens can create a very stable and loving relationship. Greens are very touchy-feely and prefer fewer boundaries. This is not true for the other personalities and it is good for Greens to realize that others express love differently. Viewing love from each of the personalities is beneficial in any relationship; however, this issue comes to light sooner for Greens. Some Greens will forever seek intense, limitless romantic connections, but others find balance and accept the romantic language that their partner speaks. Greens also need to let go of relationships that have ended. Greens will want to stay friends, but sometimes it's more important to let go. Many Greens will yearn for reunion after a partner has moved on but this will never serve them and only intensifies the abandonment issues.

As I said, Greens can be narcissistic. When they are self-centered, they manipulate through drama, erratic emotional outbursts, bossiness, and impatience. Greens are also prone to obsessive-compulsive disorders (OCD) by cycling through thought patterns when things are not going their way or when their fantasies are breaking down. This cycling can be used to distract them from their own pain and hardship. Other compulsive behaviors may be inappropriate laughter, counting random things, and other repetitive behavior. Because the Green mind moves so quickly and needs to be constantly engaged, the compulsive behavior is soothing. Greens that recognize this behavior need to know that some belief system is failing and needs to be harmonized. Experiencing OCD behavior is a cosmic 2 x 4. It's time to listen and change.

I employed a man who had a Green personality once. He earned one hundred dollars one day so I gave him a one hundred dollar bill and asked him to come back the next day. He didn't show up. Tardiness is a Green tendency, but I called him to find out where he was. He said that he had lost the hundred dollar bill and had been up all night searching for it with the flashlight. He had retraced his steps repeatedly hoping to find the money. I invited him to come back as I really needed him and told him that perhaps we'd find the money at the worksite. But he refused unable to work until he found the money. I called him at the lunch break inviting him again to come to work and assuring him that he could make another hundred dollars if he came to work. He just couldn't release the obsession and for four days he didn't sleep and searched endlessly. He could have earned $400.00 more during that time of obsessing but he was trapped by a mental mind loop that kept him from functioning.

What can the Green personality do to resolve the issues that are creating stress? The first step is to continuously be aware of the symptoms of the negative archetypes. When feeling dramatic or needy, it is imperative to cease all self-promoting behavior. This behavior takes many forms. Interrupting stories with their own self-serving stories is a dead giveaway. The more Greens sell themselves, the more insecure they feel. The more they try and feel full and good enough, the emptier they feel. The more we ego chase, the further away we get. Transformation requires doing the opposite action, connecting to the soul's perspective instead of chasing the ego's needs. The soul guides the Green personality to their true desires.

As stated earlier, one of the Green's lessons is to learn to be alone and connect internally. It is the natural ability of the Green personality to connect to its internal feelings and thoughts. They are learning to connect to the universal consciousness within them. The easiest way is to be in nature because the natural world quiets the mind and facilitates being in the present moment.

Greens have the ability to feel energy through their kinesthetic senses. It is important that the green personality stays energetically connected and one way to do this is to offers blessings over their food and water. There is a lot of research on how positive thoughts create beneficial molecular structure in food, water and plants. The tradition of offering prayers of gratitude over food is found on every continent and in nearly every religion. Greens can invite the food and to join them on the journey. A Green can rejoice and appreciate receiving the sustenance with ease. Greens can prepare meals with kindness and creativity. This is one way to create harmony with the food. In addition, prayer may benefit digestion.

Ultimately, Greens need to slow down, speak less, mono-task, decrease productivity, increase creativity, have direction but not goals, meditate, and practice Qi Gong, Tai Chi or Yoga. I favor Qi Gong because this practice awakens the kinesthetic world of energy and focuses the ability to help others. Walking through life with mindfulness, as if in meditation, also helps the Green personality. Below is a list of other recommendations.

- Set a daily feeling intention upon awakening. Decide to feel loved, energetic, peaceful or happy.
- Slow down. Use the five senses to ground if mind talk becomes too loud or rapid. Reconnect to the original intention for the day and embody that feeling.
- Receive life instead of attempting to control it. Suspend fantasy and expectation.
- Take long walks alone.
- Stop throughout the day and spend just a few minutes in meditation creating moments of pure receiving. This is the gap or the void. Do not process the moment or disappear into the future or past.
- Respect boundaries. Stay on your side of the fence and keep other people on their side of the fence.
- Wait for people to ask for help rather than imposing help on them.
- Express what you want out of relationships and see if your friends or partners want the same.

When the Green personality does this work, there will be a marked change. They become quiet, introspective, and speak wisely when asked. They become great listeners, able to enjoy solitude and the excitement of the crowd, yet are still deeply passionate about life, without the ups and downs. They will identify their effect on others, and will be considerate,

putting others' needs first. Finally, the harmonized Green will be able to have relationships come and go, still loving but without fantasy or neediness.

In my opinion, actor Robin Williams and movie director, Michael Moore, are quintessential Greens. Robin Williams transformed from the self-portrayed, intensely excitable and obsessive-compulsive Mork, from the <u>Mork & Mindy</u> sitcom, into the remarkably quick witted, calm and grounded social activist that we know today. His secondary color is Yellow, but it is proportionally much less than his Green. Williams' fellow comedians and Comic Relief participants, Billy Crystal and Whoopi Goldberg, also have Green as their primary color. Comic Relief is a charity whose mission is to "drive positive change through the power of entertainment." Creating connection via Comic Relief is one of the ways these three Greens heal the world.

Michael Moore is a Green with a secondary color of Orange. He is extremely sensitive to the needs of humanity. Initially, he was set to follow a traditional path as a minister. But the out-of-the-box thinking of the Green took him away from that journey and brought him to film making. His films give him the medium to highlight societal mistakes and suggest insightful solutions, solutions which follow the Green tenets of freedom and the power of unity.

Earvin "Magic" Johnson is the Green representative in the world of sports. Magic Johnson, with his big smile and happy-go-lucky attitude, excelled by creating magic on and off the basketball court. He also needed to be loved. He turned this need around and reinvested his money in the inner cities. The Magic Johnson Foundation includes programs that create safe productive places where inner city youth can thrive.

Paula Abdul is another Green. Her days as an <u>American Idol</u> judge are a great example. She was very emotional and touchy-feely and always had loving comments for the contestants. She strongly disliked the judgmental and unkind nature of fellow judge, Simon Cowell, a Yellow personality. She had the passion to stand up to Simon, which would have been more difficult had she been Orange.

Chapter 4

THE PATH TO BALANCE

A LIFE'S PATH IS ADORNED with infinite defining moments. These become the dramatic backdrop where we decide which beliefs we choose to keep. When we awaken to the issues that need to be harmonized, we change dramatically. *Self-remembrance* reminds us of who we can be and what the harmonized path looks like. *Awareness* is when we realize how a particular issue is the root of the vast majority of decisions in our lives. *Transition* is when we decide to change it. *Transformation* is when we choose to face our fears. Staying the same is no longer an option. We unwind the process of lamination. We replace negatives with positive experiences. How we view life instantly changes. *Transmutation* is a stage where we stop attracting the events needed to transform the old fears and belief systems. These are the steps of evolution that create emotional freedom and greater wisdom.

This harmonization process may require a total shattering of beliefs and drastic reconstruction. However, the majority of problems we need to harmonize are about finding *balance*. For example, let's look at being charitable. The word charitable indicates giving to those in need, caring for those that lack the ability to care for themselves. Yet being overly charitable may lead to over giving, not to mention enabling others and excessive self-sacrifice. This leads to self-destruction of one's identity and resentment.

There are also masculine archetypes that need to be balanced as well. The Red and Yellow personalities are achiever personalities. Both archetypes require production to feel good. Certainly in our society production is rewarded. However, the more praise that Reds and Yellows receive the more they need to produce. At some point, they need to balance being obsessively productive with just being. Green and Orange are much better

at being. These personalities, especially Orange, are viewed by society as much less industrious. They do not endeavor to produce yet are very good at being creative. In their search for balance, they need to work more to be self-sufficient without relying on others. Again, it's about balance.

One way to look at harmonizing the emotional dynamics is by balancing with the issues that create chaos. There are a minimum of three aspects to an emotion: balanced and two extremes. Micromanaging is the extreme of control. Appropriate control is the balance. Lack of control is the other extreme. Only the extremes need to be harmonized.

We commonly seek balance between the masculine and feminine personality types. Feminine personalities are focused internally. Qualities include comforting, welcoming, peacekeeping and understanding, softness and creativity. Masculine energies have an outward focus and are confrontational, logical, highly productive, and uncomfortable with vulnerability. These polar opposites must integrate the other to find balance.

For example, if someone's primary personality is Green, they will expand a Yellow aspect; the Green being feminine and Yellow being masculine. The opposite is also true. A Yellow personality will incorporate or expand Green and sometimes Orange to find balance. Yellow and Green often go together as expansive, out-of-the-box thinkers. The intuitive yellow personality will almost always have Green as a secondary color. If the Yellow personality uses shame and blame or only acknowledges information with the five senses, they will be more traditional and use Orange as a secondary personality.

Logically, having four balanced, equally intense personality types is ideal. I've discovered that older subjects have more balanced results on the personality test. Also, people often choose spouses who mirror the personality trait they lack. For example, if our two primary colors are Green and Yellow with a little Red in the background, most of our romantic relationships will be Orange, likely Orange with Red as the secondary color. We simply need to learn how to speak and feel orangeness. Our romantic partner would have the opposite component. This is the relational superglue needed while we both learn to appreciate the opposite qualities. Love keeps couples connected long enough to bridge the differences and create change. It's how relationships work.

In any good relationship the partners become more like each other as time goes by, thus achieving balance. If we do not deeply understand or become more like our partner, it is difficult for the relationship to stay healthy. Relationships are made to meet in the middle. The relationship might be tumultuous at times, but that is all part of the path towards balance and inner peace. All of our relationships are carefully crafted to either reflect our issues or to find a balance. A person without balance will have a life filled with unhappiness, emptiness, and stress. Balance is the path of self-acceptance, acceptance of others and acceptance of life as it is. The work is to transform fear into wonder. This allows us to move through our so-called terrible experiences with improved outcome and even enjoyment.

One of the characteristics of the balanced path is that we *receive* life instead of manipulating life. Manipulation equals exhaustion as the ego attempts to control everyone and everything. The ego manipulates, the soul receives. The ego serves only itself. It has great intelligence but lacks wisdom. It lacks connection with anything that doesn't yield personal payoffs. It screams for deregulation so that it can get everything it wants. The ego needs laws, for it lacks the ability to hear creation's moral acumen. The ego dwells in an insular disconnected world, unable to allow acceptance, wholeness, or the oneness that leads to decisions that serve humanity.

The soul embodies consciousness that sees beyond time and is aided by universal wisdom. Our souls are individuated from the Creator, but not disconnected from the Source. Our connection to our soul consciousness is our greatest guide. Discerning our action motivations is essential when we are helping others on their harmonization path. The balanced path must be walked individually in order to harmonize the whole.

Chapter 5

A MYSTICAL STORY

Rabbi Rami Shapiro writes, " The ancient Rabbis taught 'God desires the heart.' The eighteenth-century Jewish revivalist movement called Hasidism was one of these heart swings." The founder of this movement was Israel ben Eliezer (1698-1760), who came to be called the Besht, an acronym for Ba'al Shem Tov, Master of the Good Name. There are many stories documenting his life and his teaching but this tale in particular gave me an understanding about living life with balance. I hope that it reawakens your strength and love of the journey, as it has mine.

When the Ba'al Shem Tov was five years old, his father lay dying. His father shared a secret with a boy, the most important lesson that a parent can impart to their child. He told the boy that he was already whole within, that his soul was complete, invulnerable and pure. He said that although the Evil One would surround him his entire life, there was no way for the Evil One to damage his soul. The father explained that this Evil One surrounds everyone. It holds, distracts, and makes humanity feel bored, anxious, or frustrated. But the secret is that the soul is pure. No matter what happens, the soul cannot be damaged by others.

When his father died, Israel became an orphan having lost his mother when he was only eight days old. The people of the town took the boy in and sent him to school. But young Israel couldn't stand being cooped up inside a building listening to teachers while the woods, rivers, sky, flowers and animals waited outside. So the boy walked in the woods, week after week, year after year. This is where he received his education: from the critters, the trees and the sound of the river.

One day, when Israel was nine-years-old, the schoolmaster asked him to escort the young neighborhood children to class. Young Israel agreed. He gathered the younger children, as if he was the Pied Piper of Hamlin, though he was only nine-years-old himself. Instead of taking a direct route, Young Israel guided them through the woods and into the field, teaching them all along the way to school. Then Israel taught them a song. We don't know the exact words but it went something like, "Hallelujah, praise God, Amen." So the children walked to school singing their hallelujahs.

Well, when innocent voices sing songs of praise to the Divine, a crack is opened in the dark clouds so little bits of the song flow through. It was said that this stirred the Divine Presence and that maybe the time had come for the great change in the world to take place. A new level of consciousness had been achieved.

At the same time, the Evil One that lived on the other side of the heavens realized something was happening. This something interfered with his job, which was to keep people exactly where they were or worse. So the Evil One went to the Divine Source and said, "I need to strive against these children."

The Divine One replied, "Strive you must." The Divine One knows that the only way to achieve higher consciousness is through free will so permission was granted to the Evil One to do whatever it needed, to see what would happen.

The Evil One went down to earth to search for an evil assistant. It went to all the creatures in the field and forest. It went to the plants. It went to the insects. It went to the birds. Each time it said, "I would like you to help me because I need to do something to defeat young Israel who is causing trouble in the heavens."

The creatures refused the request because they all loved Israel. They were his friends and none of them would work hand in hand with the Evil One. Finally, the Evil One found a creature willing to work with it. It was the charcoal maker. Unfortunately, the charcoal maker was not given a soul. Sometimes someone is born without a soul. They look human, but in reality, they are just a pitiful creature. Oftentimes, the charcoal maker grew fangs, and hair on his arms. Though he never attacked anyone, he always scared people by his presence. In fact, the charcoal maker was actually a werewolf. One day when the Evil One found him asleep, he pulled out the charcoal maker's heart and placed his own heart, the heart of darkness, into the creature.

Soon Israel led the children to school, singing "Hallelujah, praise God, Amen." The dark creature with fangs and fire dripping from his eyes loomed at the edge of the woods and when the children saw him, they were terrified as they looked up at the monster, whose fangs grew longer by the minute. Some of the children fainted while others ran for their lives. Young Israel looked at the creature, then at the children. He ran around gathering the children together as the creature disappeared into the woods.

The children ran home and told their parents about the creature. The parents said, "No more, Young Israel. You're not going to lead our children anymore. It's too dangerous."

But Young Israel, the Ba'al Shem Tov, knew in his heart the lesson his father taught him. No matter how great the surrounding evil, the soul within is pure. He told the people in the village, "Your souls are pure and nothing can touch the depth of your being." He went around and pleaded with them, saying, "Please let me take the children to school tomorrow morning.

The parents agreed.

The next day Young Israel gathered the children for their walk to school. It was hard for them to sing because they were so frightened, but they sang anyway. As they got close to the edge of the woods, the Ba'al Shem Tov turned to them and said, "Stay here and let me go ahead." He turned and entered the first row of trees. Sure enough, the dark beast loomed before him. It grew taller and taller like a cloud of darkness. The Ba'al Shem Tov slowly walked forward and the werewolf became even more terrifying. Yet Israel continued until he was right in front of the blackest of black, the heart of evil, the heart of darkness. And as he stood there, he whispered, "The soul is pure. The soul is pure." Surely the darkness would have overwhelmed him had he not been whispering this mantra.

Young Israel reached in and held the heart of darkness and saw one drop of blood oozing from this heart. The blood dropped into Israel's open palm. Immediately, he was touched in the compassionate center of his being, for he knew the loneliness of evil. Evil cannot feel the spark of holiness deep within. Evil cannot feel one with the Divine. In that moment of compassion, the Ba'al Shem Tov placed the heart on the ground and instantly the earth split open and swallowed the heart of darkness.

The Ba'al Shem Tov went back and led his children to the school. The next day, the townspeople found the old charcoal maker dead in the bushes. From that time on there were never any problems with the werewolf/charcoal maker. It was recorded that even though the Ba'al Shem Tov was able to take the children to school, they never again sang like the first time. The darkness that lives in the center of the earth breathed out fear, doubt and self-criticism that have kept humanity from fully expressing the freedom of their being.

The End

When we realize that our soul is whole, there is no room for fear. The charcoal maker was without a soul. Because of this, evil could easily insert its dark heart into this being and manipulate its every action, its every thought. This tale reminds us that the more we are separated from our soul, the more evil and fear run our lives. The more we forget that our souls are pure and unchangeable by those around us, the more we become sheep or zombies doing the Evil One's bidding. The symptoms of this are clear. When others manipulate us with stories of societal evil, how quickly do fear, anger and hostility rise within us? How quickly do we run to feelings of harm, terror and the wish to eliminate our enemy? How quickly do we become soldiers willing to battle to the death against our foes? How much persuading does it take for us to hate one another? Fear and evil are extensions of one another. This is the brokenness that exists within humanity. Healing this break is our work.

I am reminded of the Hebrew word "yirah." This word can be translated to mean "fear" but it can also mean "awe." For example, Psalm 86:11 uses this word and could be translated as either "Teach me in Your way God; I will walk in Your truth; let my heart be undivided in fear of Your name" or it could be translated as "let my heart be in awe of Your name." Those two definitions are at opposite ends of the emotional spectrum.

Yirah splits humanity and the work is to move from fear to awe. To move into awe, we must contact our soul and its wisdom. We must realize our oneness which equals acceptance, tolerance, love, patience, forgiveness, grace, inner peace, joy, hopefulness and kindness. The symptoms of fear are the opposite and include thoughts and acts of violence.

When we live in awe/reverence, there is no need for fear, yet fear can be the gateway to our issues. Fear is omnipresent and self-generating. We can't blame an external force when we don't feel good enough because this feeling is a result of losing ourselves. This is why we work to transform the emotional dynamics of chaos into harmony.

The Ba'al Shem Tov, Young Israel is well named. The word Israel means "one who wrestles with the Divine." He knew his soul was pure and could not be changed by evil, yet he still had to reassure himself as he walked into the heart of darkness. The good news is that this mantra, "my soul is pure," can remind us to feel whole. The story is rich with descriptions of how fear grows and amplifies the closer we get. Fear is always bigger than reality. This is when we create reasons why we should not confront the fear. Actually, the more we fear something, the more we must embrace it because fear guides us to the issue we need to work on. Of course, there is a difference between fear and anxiety in the emotional realm, and normal fears. I am not advocating we jump out of a plane if we fear death.

The story also teaches that we can learn much about ourselves by being in nature and being with animals. This is a fundamental principle shared with Taoism. By watching and listening to all that exists within nature, we learn everything we need to know. When I take long walks in the forest I am always amazed by my internal journey, where I really listen to my inner wisdom. This is where I connect with animals, plants and myself. We don't always need books, but we always need nature.

The story also points out that evil is a part of creation. The Evil One, or Satan, must go to the Divine One to ask permission to carry out his greater purpose. This means that the obstacle, the emotional baggage, is a tool for us to practice free will. Overcoming fears fosters growth. Expanding past our fear replaces chaos with peace. This is the path to harmony. The Ba'al Shem Tov's greatest moment of compassion was for

Satan because he knew he was disconnected from the Divine in order to do the work of evil. When this occurs, there is no feeling of joy or sense of Oneness.

There is a wonderful gnostic Christian writing, accredited to Jesus, in the Gospel of Thomas. "If you bring forth what is within you, what you bring forth will save you. If you do not bring forth what is within you, what you do not bring forth will destroy you" (Gospel of Thomas 70). This means that our issues, as well as our soul, reside within. If we do not access our soul, our life's work and our radical uniqueness, the things that bring chaos and stress will destroy us. When we remove the ego's debilitating and controlling emotional filters, we access all of ourselves. This creates our life of awe. This will save us.

Chapter 6

THE BASIC FOUR AND MORE

THIS CHAPTER CONTAINS The Basic Four guidelines for understanding the life journey. This chapter, along with the Chapter 7, are some of the E3 philosophies that will help you create a harmonized path.

GUIDELINE 1: SHOW UP

Many of us live in small, tightly confined environments that we don't often venture out of. We create safe spaces, both physical and mental, to exert control of things around us. Showing up means to wake up every day to find the hidden potential that waits. Showing up is to be aware of the depth of every moment and every decision. It means feeling all feelings, all of them, not just the positive ones. It means really tasting food, feeling the breeze, watching clouds churn through the sky and enjoying the laughter of children. When we show up, we spend a lot more time saying "yes" instead of "no." We engage our fears and explore them instead of hiding from them. What keeps us from showing up is fear of the unknown. Show up.

GUIDELINE 2: TELL THE TRUTH

These three little words can be life's greatest struggle. Much of the time, we pretend to be something that we're not. Many of us try to persuade ourselves that we are either more or better than we fear and some of us take the other road and continuously put ourselves down. Neither of these are the truth. Telling the truth means not only telling the truth to others, but also telling the truth to ourselves. Ask yourself the following questions. Am I really being who I am or am I presenting a façade so that people will accept me? Am I authentic?

GUIDELINE 3: DO YOUR BEST

Doing your best means squeezing possibilities from every effort and experience. It means leaving no stone unturned and knowing that you did the best you could in any particular moment. Every moment reveals new information so holding ourselves responsible for the things we discovered after the fact is self-destructive. If we made a choice that didn't turn out the way we wished, that's okay. The point is that we made a choice and stayed in the game. The next step is to get the most out of the experience. Not doing our best job leads to regret and wondering, "If I had done more or followed my heart, what would life be like today?" We often associate a bad choice with struggle. Struggle is the place of the greatest lessons. Don't be surprised if past choices turned out not to have been the best ones. Lessons give us the tools to see and do things differently. This is what creates wisdom. Doing everything as fully as we can, as if it were the last chance, is the path to a full life.

GUIDELINE 4: BE UNATTACHED TO THE OUTCOME

We lament and cycle through thoughts of how things would be if only they had gone our way. Staying connected to unfulfilled wishes, fantasies and beating ourselves up over unrealized expectations never serves us. Enjoying what is in front of us is the only course of action that makes sense. It also leads to getting the most out of the new circumstances – regardless of outcome. Integrating and adapting the information learned allows us to show up, tell the truth and do the best we can in the next experience.

There are two ways to look at every experience. One is to look through the eyes of the ego. This is a world that sees things as wins or losses. Getting the upper hand, coming out on top, and winning are all ways in which the ego looks at an event. This ego game starts when two people socialize and start slipping in information to puff themselves up. Comparing attributes and insecurities is almost automatic. When looking through the ego's eyes, it is very hard to find our highest and best path.

The alternative is to see through the eyes of the soul. There is not one situation in life that the soul regrets. It has animated into a physical life to gather events and harmonize the chaos within. It coordinates experiences that the ego chooses to run away from. These experiences often bring out our insecurities and fears. In order to move beyond them, the soul knows it must walk through them with open arms. It must learn to experience the event in neutrality. It does not wish to blame others or collapse to a negative or dysfunctional archetype that keeps transformation from occurring.

Without this choice, the cyclic maze of the ego is inescapable. The ego wants to even the score through gossip and revenge when it loses the comparison game. It is in these manifested situations that the soul encourages us to learn and adapt. Ultimately, this is the only road that makes sense. The patient soul directs our life to the same events until we choose the highest path leading to a smoother life. This is how we harmonize chaos. Letting go of bitterness allows life's sweetness to flow. I call this the highest and best path and I describe this way of being in the following way:

- Experience the event.
- Feel the experience without using negative archetypes or name-calling.
- Adapt to the new parameters looking for any positive lessons you can learn.
- Function and return to getting the most out of the experience or your life possible.

This chapter is named the Basic Four and More because there are so many philosophies and practices that can help to harmonize the chaos in our lives and lead us on a path of greater harmony and peace. We find the following sensible, simple two examples in the Buddhist tradition.

The Three Poisons are Greed, Hate and Delusion but my Buddhist teacher interpreted them and taught them to me as Grasping, Aversion, and Ignorance.

Grasping. This is the ego chasing after what we desire. But what we desire covers up the fears and insecurities that the ego runs from. For most of us, this incorporates the majority of our daily actions. We may be best served by adopting a practice of not wanting. This may help is to separate grasping from wanting to experience a life of unbridled joy, without a secondary payoff to the ego.

Aversion. This is pushing things away. However, the more we push things away, the more entangled with these things we become. When aversion is based on anger towards others, aversion stimulates the laws of attraction. The more we hate someone, the more we see that behavior in people around us. Oftentimes we'll see someone that looks like the person we wish to avoid. We may begin looking in every crowd to see if that person might be there. Clearly, we are more connected to them now than ever before. Aversion is the mechanism in which we create shadows within ourselves. Shadows are the things or thought we dislike about ourselves. They often don't fit in with our morals or belief systems and we avoid or bury them deep inside. But it is there that they fester waiting to erupt, often manifesting as extreme behaviors. It is for these reasons that the path to harmonization does not include aversion. We must listen to and work through the things we wish to hide from.

Ignorance. This could be described as forgetting that we are spiritual beings in a physical form, not physical beings in a spiritual experience. Nothing in life makes any sense unless we see that there is a bigger whole that we are part of. The only thing that gives us persistent happiness is the de-junking of our emotional baggage. This is the harmonizing of our life and this is what we do. Chaos is the things that make us angry, stressful, and fearful. This internal chaos is reflected in negative emotional dynamics and takes us away from our God-like side. We have the capacity to scoop the chaos out of creation and harmonize it. When we harmonize these feelings, we also harmonize our personal environment. Unfortunately, we often lose sight of the fact that we are an integral part of creation. This is our ignorance.

The second Buddhist concept is beautifully simple. Your soul will put in front of you the experiences that will aid you in your growth and change. The philosophy encompasses these three things:

Do what you enjoy.

Do what you're good at or what is in your nature.

Do what comes to you or is in front of you.

We often depart from this road even though it makes good sense. We are disappointed when we lose ourselves and the path but if we believe that the soul directs our life by creating healthy circumstances, it also directs us to a rewarding life. This simple road inevitably leads to happiness.

Chapter 7

THE TWENTY-FIVE PRINCIPLES

These principles will help you navigate your life and the lives of the people you are helping. They are guidelines to recreate a path that is smooth, without negative repercussions. You will find your own guiding principles as you do this work. Please add them to the list.

PRINCIPLE ONE: THE PRINCIPLE OF CYCLES.

Life has a cyclical nature. The issues that you see today you have seen before and you will see again.

PRINCIPLE TWO: THE PRINCIPLE OF INERTIA.

Before you change your behaviors or engage in the fears of your life, you will come up with a very logical and often noble reason not to change.

PRINCIPLE THREE: THE PRINCIPLE OF WISDOM.

Don't be surprised if the person that you feel is harming you the most is actually saving (or shaping) your life. They are directing your attention to what needs to be healed.

PRINCIPLE FOUR: THE PRINCIPLE OF ATTRACTION.

We attract and create what we give the most energy to. The vast majority of our thoughts are in the subconscious mind. This is the chaos that hides fear.

Principle Five: THE PRINCIPLE OF SUBCONSCIOUS MANIFESTING.

You must be okay not having before having. The fear of lack can be so strong that you continue attracting lack instead of the situations and objects you desire. You must accept yourself as you are. Only then do you allow yourself to manifest the things you want.

Principle Six: THE PRINCIPLE OF SELF-ACCEPTANCE.

Accept yourself. What you use to bolster your ego will eventually be gone. If you don't want to lose abilities or possessions, learn to be okay with who you are.

Principle Seven: THE PRINCIPLE OF 99%.

99% of the horrible things in your life have never happened. In other words, 99% of your fears live in your mind, not the physical world. However, these fears will be perceived by the body as if they really occurred.

Principle Eight: THE PRINCIPLE OF FEAR VERSUS AWE.

If you do one thousand things right and one thing wrong, focusing on the one wrong thing will keep you in a state of fear. But if you focus on all the things you did right, you are in a state of awe.

Principle Nine: THE PRINCIPLE OF MIRRORING.

Our issues tend to surface when we are around someone with the same issues. An example is control meets control.

Principle Ten: THE PRINCIPLE OF ONENESS HEALING.

The sins of the parent become the sins of the children. (The Hebrew word sin translates to missing the mark, a definition without guilt.) The healing of the child can become the healing of the parents. The healing of the parents can become the healing of the grandparents and so on.

Principle Eleven: THE PRINCIPLE OF THE SWORD.

Live by the sword die by the sword. If you use a tool or weapon to control others then you are susceptible to the same tool or weapon being used on you. If you do not use these techniques then you are immune to others using them on you. Judgment and guilt are weapons of the ego.

Principle Twelve: THE PRINCIPLE OF THE UNSPOKEN CONTRACT.

Our actions with others reflect what we want in return. We treat others the way we want to be treated.

Principle Thirteen: THE PRINCIPLE OF REFRAMING.

It is always possible to go back and reframe your actions and your words in a more harmonious way. It doesn't matter how much time has passed, reframing always has power. Some of our greatest healings occur on our deathbed. Practice reframing in your mind's eye first to amplify the power.

Principle Fourteen: THE PRINCIPLE OF EQUALITY.

No one is better and no one is worse. We are all the same. We are all connected. We are oneness.

Principle Fifteen: THE PRINCIPLE OF GOOD ENOUGH.

Nearly all the issues of our life boil down to control and good enough. Venture deep into why you wish to control others and you'll reach the fear of not being good enough.

Principle Sixteen: THE PRINCIPLE OF THE PURE SOUL.

The soul is invincible, pure, and whole.

PRINCIPLE SEVENTEEN: THE PRINCIPLE OF READINESS.

You are never given a lesson that you do not have the tools to overcome.

PRINCIPLE EIGHTEEN: THE PRINCIPLE OF MOVING FORWARD.

Fear is always bigger than reality. The closer we get to releasing the fear and its underlying beliefs, the more fear grows. It can paralyze us, but knowing this and seeing the pattern allows us the freedom to move through it.

PRINCIPLE NINETEEN: THE PRINCIPLE OF WHAT IS.

Do not fear a changing future. We are capable of creating great sadness and loss by fantasizing and anticipating what the future holds. Don't grieve over a future that never materialized. Fantasies rarely turn out the way you dreamed. Enjoy what is, and forget what is not.

PRINCIPLE TWENTY: THE PRINCIPLE OF THE FENCE.

Stay on your side of the fence and mind your own business. It's much more restful. When you have mastered staying on your side of the fence, it's easier to keep others on their side.

PRINCIPLE TWENTY-ONE: THE PRINCIPLE OF SIMPLICITY.

Keep it simple. The greatest source of power in the universe comes from the simplest, most elemental things. The more you can see miracles in their simplest form, the more potential you have for enjoying the wonder of life.

PRINCIPLE TWENTY-TWO: THE PRINCIPLE OF INNER PEACE.

Some people say they can't change but everything is changeable. The door to inner peace is locked from the inside. You must understand what best serves your higher self. Stop allowing your ego to make decisions.

PRINCIPLE TWENTY-THREE: THE PRINCIPLE OF MARTYRDOM.

When things don't go as planned, keep your feelings from transforming into blame or revenge. To avoid becoming a martyr or victim, all one needs to do is to perceive, feel, adapt, live and let go of needing to be right!

PRINCIPLE TWENTY-FOUR: THE PRINCIPLE OF FREE WILL.

Initially, we create our habits and then our habits create us. Sometimes we forget that we created the beliefs and habits. We can use our free will to amend them at any time. You made them and you can change them.

PRINCIPLE TWENTY-FIVE: THE PRINCIPLE OF THE CHASE.

The more we chase, the further we get from what we truly crave. The goals of the ego are an illusion. The soul's vision is the clear picture, the real stuff.

PRINCIPLE TWENTY-SIX: THE PRINCIPLE OF CHANGE.

When the path is not working, the best thing to do is usually the opposite.

PART II

Chapter 8

MUSCLE TESTING STEP BY STEP

ANY MUSCLE CAN BE USED for the testing, but the muscle group most commonly used is the arm abductors, primarily the deltoid. This is the group of muscles that lifts the arm out to the side and up over the head. The starting position for the arm is straight out at the side at a 90° angle to the body.

Next, the arm is internally rotated to where the thumb is pointing downward. The arm must never bend at the elbow. Muscle testing gauges the subject's ability to maintain this arm position while the tester presses down on the wrist or forearm. Again, make sure that the thumb is pointing downward. The tester applies just the amount of pressure so that the muscle resists being pushed down. First, assess a strong muscle.

A strong muscle should be able to hold the arm in position solidly against resistance without shaking or giving way. This testing is not about brute strength and trying to overpower the muscle. The point is to find out the amount of strength needed so that the subject can still resist with a solid arm feel. The right amount of pressure is when pressing 15% to 20% more causes the arm to become overpowered and drop towards the ground.

Athletic men and women will have greater upper body strength than non-athletic men and women. Determine and adjust the maximum functional amount of pressure for the test, where the subject's arm can remain at a 90° angle to their body. Give consistent pressure so that the client is actively resisting. This also gives the client confidence in the validity of the results..

The next step is to find out what a weak muscle test feels like. It is the contrast between strong and weak that gives affirmative or negative results. Think of it like this: an affirmative test means this line of questioning has the greatest probability of being true or beneficial. When a muscle goes weak as a result of a question, it may feel like you are applying less pressure. It is hard for client to believe that you are giving the same amount of pressure. They will think you are pushing harder as their arms just drops. This is the reason for consistency. You can also ask clients to sense the pressure of your fingers on their arm. This proves to them how little pressure is applied when their arm is weak, and how much more pressure is applied when their arm is strong. The muscle testing steps are explained in greater detail, below.

STEP ONE: CREATE A SACRED SPACE AND SET YOUR INTENTIONS

It is very important for the tester to check their intentions and motivations before starting a session. One can set their intention by inhaling, affirming that you are there for the client, and then exhaling slowly. This technique opens doors deep within the subject, oftentimes revealing vulnerabilities and sensitivities so regard this interaction as sacred. If the motivation is solely to help that person, information will come quickly and accurately. But if there is an underlying agenda, belief system, or theory being advocated, the subject will sense this and the muscle testing will shut down. If working from a place of performance or ego, the test will not work either. The muscle will not go weak, but will simply stay strong and no information will be gleaned.

If a tester is fear based, worrying about being inadequate or unskilled, the muscle test will not work. The tester's insecure energy inhibits the ability to do this work and the results will be unreliable. Practitioners of this technique must be willing to jump right in without worry of perfection, and focus on the intention of helping another human being to the best of their ability. Employing this technique requires neutrality and acceptance and the more a technique is practiced, the more reliable the information. Stay with the process and concentrate on creating a sacred feeling of trust and acceptance with your subject.

STEP TWO: POSITION AND TEST

As previously stated, the correct testing position is for the subject to hold the arm out to the side of the body at a 90° angle, with the arm internally rotated so that the thumb is pointing towards the ground. Place one or two fingers on the subject's distal forearm, just proximal to the wrist.

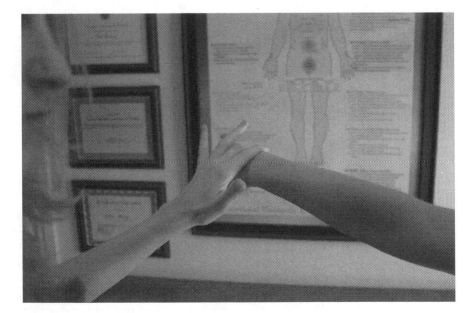

Picture 2

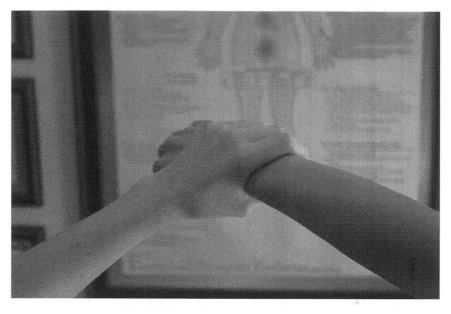

Picture 3

It is important that you do not grab the wrist but only maintain contact with two fingers. The subject can relax and be able to resist the testing pressure without feeling dominated. Maintaining this kind of finger-only pressure serves as a reminder that you are only interested in the truth and are not invested in the outcome. Objectivity and neutrality will be a challenge for any tester who assumes the correct answer. Staying neutral avoids the temptation to elicit a specific result. It is vital that you continue to focus on helping the subject realize change and healing. It is imperative to divest one's ego and self-esteem from the test outcome.

STEP THREE: TEST

Place one or two fingers on the top of the subject's distal forearm while standing near the subject's arm. Do not stand directly in front of the subject; otherwise you will be at a biomechanical strength disadvantage as shown in Picture 4.

Picture 4.

Stand close enough to the subject's arm so you do not have to strain. This gives you greater sensitivity and feel for the result. Be aware that when some subjects sense they are "losing" at the muscle test, they recruit other muscle groups or employ tactics to shore up their strength. The most common is to flex the elbow and recruit the bicep muscle to assist. They may also flex their body to the opposite side to hold up the arm or externally rotate the arm to where the thumb is no longer pointing towards the ground, as seen in Picture 5.

Picture 5.

If any of these compensations happen, gently ask them to keep their arm straight and to stay in a normal posture. Explain your wish to help and that it is important they hold their arm in the same position each time for the muscle test to be accurate.

STEP FOUR: DETERMINE WEAK AND STRONG

Before testing you must ascertain normal arm strength. Place your fingers on the subject's forearm and ask the subject to hold against your resistance. Press down about half an inch. The subject will start lifting their arm into your testing hand. This gives the subject time to engage the muscles fully. Press down just a little bit more to feel the strength of that arm. The arm should not shake or give way. If it does, you are pressing too hard. Remember, you are only looking for that solid feel. Be certain to press hard enough so that you don't get a false positive when testing for a weak muscle. In other words, if you don't press down hard enough, a weak muscle won't give way. You must use the same pressure each time, enough for a strong muscle to resist and a weak muscle to yield.

Determine what a weak muscle feels like by placing the index finger of your non-pushing hand at the top of the subject's nose, between the eyebrows.

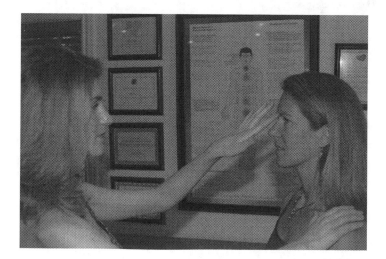

Picture 6.

This indentation is called the glabella. When you place your finger slowly and gently on the glabella, and then push down on the subject's arm, it should elicit a weak arm response. If the arm magically goes weak, you're touching the glabella. Take your finger off this point and retest the arm muscle strength. The muscle will return to strong. The contrast of the two is not only valuable information for you as the tester, but it is important for the subject to see and feel the difference.

I commonly ask subjects to feel the pressure of my fingers on their arm. I want the subject to realize that I am not pressing harder, creating the weak response, or less hard to create a strong response. In fact, I press significantly harder when the arm is strong so that they truly get how hard I am pressing. When I touch the glabella, known as the polarity point, the pressure used on the forearm is significantly less. It is powerful when both tester and subject feel the difference, because it makes the test results believable and the subject will be compelled to follow through on the information gleaned.

Many wonder why touching the glabella helps with muscle testing. Pointing to this spot is like pointing directly at the hypothalamus, pituitary and pineal glands, and the limbic center of the brain. The hypothalamus, pituitary, and limbic center are the core emotional centers of the brain. The pineal gland was once considered the ancient eye of primitive fish, but has evolved and is credited with monitoring the length of daytime hours and giving input to our circadian rhythms. When we touch the glabella, we seem to connect to these areas. This is one of those many cases that we know works, but are unable to validate absolutely.

If you are unable to elicit the weak muscle response when touching the glabella polarity point, it is important to assess the following factors: hydration, patient fears and anxiety, presence of pungent chemicals or odors, as well as your own anxiety, intention, and hydration. These can all affect the muscle testing result. If you come in too fast with your finger on the glabella or press too hard the patient might feel threatened and will shut down.

Picture 7.

I cannot stress the importance of proper hydration. Ninety percent of the time, difficulty eliciting the weak muscle response occurs because the subject is dehydrated. People are generally chronically dehydrated. My friend, who is a gerontologist, tells me that the number one issue for his senior patients is dehydration and all the health consequences it brings. Have a tall glass of water nearby while doing muscle testing because at least half of the people will need to drink water before starting. Most patients must continue to drink water during testing, especially when dealing with deeper emotional issues. There is a large scientific database regarding the capacities of water and how it stores and carries human thoughts and feelings. If everything is staying strong during your testing, meaning there are no questions to which a weak muscle response is elicited, recheck the polarity point at the glabella. If you cannot get a weak response, it's time for more water.

If after hydration, a weak muscle response still can't be found, try the cross crawl.

Have the subject get on their hands and knees, then lift the right arm out straight in front while extending the left leg behind. The arm and opposing leg should be in line with the body and parallel to the ground.

Return the client to the all fours position and repeat on the opposite side, alternating about ten times. The crawling reflex may reboot the brain.

Picture 8.

Picture 9.

A subject's generalized fear and anxiety as well as stress about the muscle testing procedure can hinder test results. Take some time to calm the client before beginning, gently explaining your intentions and hopes for the session, emphasizing strongly that you want to help the client. You may even play a little game asking the subject to say his or her name, and then test the arm strength. It will typically be strong. Then have the person say "My name is Barney Rubble," or "My name is Wilma Flintstone." The muscle will become demonstrably weak. This is when the client can laugh and relax, and you can proceed. You may also do some food testing for allergy or tolerance to show the client how easy and useful the technique is. By the time you have reassured the subject or played a little game, muscle testing should be working again.

If the tests still are not working, check your intentions again. It is important that your only intention is to help the person. You do not want to be invested in the outcome of the muscle test for fear you could lead the person's response. When I began muscle testing, I'd silently state, "I want the truth." This set my intention and reminded me to not be attached to the outcome of the test. This enabled me to focus on applying consistent pressure in each muscle test. If you feel that you have failed or used the wrong concept, your muscle tests and your ability to help will be less effective. Stay neutral at all times.

Occasion I have been in a room with someone who is wearing a lot of perfume or hairspray. This may overload a sensitive person and make it difficult to test. Additionally, if the person you are testing has been around pungent or toxic chemicals, this too can cause the person to shut down. In general, anything that is shocking or that can trigger the fight or flight reflex can shut someone down.

Finally, there may come a time in a session when the individual being tested signals that enough has been done for the day. You don't want to dilute the big messages received with too many other emotional dynamics. What typically happens is that the muscle testing will only elicit a strong response despite water, cross crawling, or any other technique. This signals that enough is enough. Trust in this wisdom. If unsure, test the concept, "We are good for today." If the muscle test is affirmative, then you know you have done your job for the day. Let the client process what has come up.

STEP FIVE: INTERPRET RESULTS

How can you tell when a muscle test is affirmative (a "yes") or negative (a "no")? In other words, when are you on track and when you are off track?

Have the subject make statements that you know are true such as "I am okay with receiving love from my partner." If these questions are all affirmative, this means you are on track, you will get a strong muscle test. It is almost like a lie detector test. When people tell the truth, their body stays strong. When lying, their body becomes weak.

However, when the tester makes the statements, the opposite is true. If you say, "Let's test the concept that this job is in your highest and best interest," or "Let's test the concept that you are okay receiving love from your partner," the affirmative or on track statement will lead to a weak muscle. Conversely, a negative or off track statement will lead to the muscle staying strong. Keeping the differences straight is the only complexity in muscle testing and may be difficult at first. Simply stated, when you make statements, a weak muscle is the affirmative result. A strong muscle is the negative. The muscle test will occasionally come out exactly opposite to the above description. Test results will come out exactly opposite to the above description. This is the phenomenon of being "switched." Usually, this can be rectified by doing the cross crawl exercise outlined above. To check this, make a simple statement, "give me an affirmative test." Then ask for a negative test. You can then correlate weakness or strength to on track or off track.

The innate is a concept within chiropractic philosophy. Think of the innate as an inner consciousness that wants you to live in good health. The innate or subconscious mind is very cooperative. It will adapt to your belief system regarding which test should create a weak versus a strong muscle. There are various spin-off techniques of applied kinesiology. In some of these techniques, muscle weakness means an affirmative test. In others, a strong muscle denotes an affirmative test. It would be nice if everything was black and white. But the adaptability of the innate helps create flexibility so that many systems can work. Ultimately, the intention of consciousness is to access the information that each one of us needs to help and transform ourselves. The flexibility of the E3 technique may seem complex and difficult to grasp. However, the more you work with this system, the more you'll appreciate and harvest its vast wisdom. When you feel lost, ask a question and the innate will lead you to the answer. When in doubt ask, "Give me an affirmative and give me a negative." You'll immediately find out which correlates to strong and which correlates to weak.

It is important to ask permission of this innate consciousness for access to certain questions. The muscle testing will not work and the information will not be clear if the line of questioning is not in the subject's highest and best interest. If this occurs, simply ask "Can I ask the question about ____?" In the E3 process, if the muscle goes weak access is granted. If the muscle stays strong then you must leave this line of questioning alone.

The following examples will illustrate this concept. People often want to know about the future, everything from knowing the Super Bowl results to choosing winning lottery numbers. These questions are usually asked for the benefit of the ego, to obtain money, power or advancement. This information may not be in the highest and best interest of the subject because many people who win large sums of money end up losing it and regret winning it in the first place. Another example is when inquiring about a third party who is not present at the session. The tester needs to ask permission, even if the intentions of the question are pure and beneficial.

The E3 technique does probe into the future; however, it is important to remember that the answers are only probabilities and not fate. The closer you get to the time of the events, the greater the probability your answers will come true. Future outcomes are based on a lifetime or even lifetimes of decisions. Hundreds, if not thousands of choices, will lead one down a certain path. The more we make a certain decision, the more likely we are to repeat it. When we look back at our choices, it seems inevitable that we ended up being where we are. This is why the Greek philosopher Heraclitus said, "A man's character is his fate." Thank goodness that free will exists or we might forever be stuck cyclically repeating the same actions.

There are strategies that will lead to greater accuracy in your muscle testing. The questions asked will be interpreted quite literally so if just one part of a complex statement is off track, everything in that statement will show up as off track. For example, I might ask a subject, "I would like to test the concept that your mother, your father and your greatest enemy all love you very much." The mother and father no doubt love the subject very much, but combining concepts in this complex statement causes the muscle test to deem this statement off track. Ask questions that test only one concept at a time.

There are times when the muscle feels half weak. The arm is shaky and releases, but does not collapse as on weak responses. This is the innate telling you that you're on track, but not quite right. Fine tune your concept by using more precise wording or more specific descriptions. Stay with it until that muscle is truly weak and you have distilled the most truthful statement.

As a chiropractor, I used muscle tests to ascertain which spinal segments had issues and to test for food allergies and intolerances. When I touched the injured or sensitive area, or a problem food or allergen was introduced, the muscle would test as weak. I then moved from the physical to the psychological-emotional realm, and in doing so, questioned the origins of this information. This is part of the great mystery of the universe. All I know is that the guidance comes from a sentient perspective or consciousness. When we recruit its help it knows when a certain line of questioning is beneficial or not. This consciousness knows which issues must be discussed first before the next issue will make sense. It knows just how to organize the issues for the maximum therapeutic benefit. I have found over the years that the best I can do is to get out of the way and let the consciousness guide the process.

Chapter 9

MUSCLE TESTING APPLICATIONS

THERE ARE MANY WAYS IN which you can use muscle testing. When you ask the client questions and the muscle remains strong, it is a negative test and no information is gained. But if the muscle strength changes and the arm becomes shaky, weak, or drops, this indicates you have found something or you are on the right track.

Therapy localization is the technique to determine which area requires treatment. The tester touches the area of the body in question with one hand while performing a muscle test with the other. If the muscle test is weak, it signifies a positive test and indicates this is an area of dysfunction. The area is checked following treatment, and when the muscle test becomes strong, the treatment is complete.

Muscle testing can also help determine which type of treatment is necessary using the technique of two pointing. The area of dysfunction, determined through therapy localization, is point one. While continuing to touch that area, the tester will introduce the verbal concept of a possible treatment modality (point two). If the muscle test becomes strong in response, this indicates that the treatment is correct. If the muscle stays weak, verbally introduce the next treatment modality and keep repeating until the muscle test becomes strong and the correct treatment is determined.

Muscle testing is particularly helpful in determining if nutritional supplements are indicated. As stated above, when you use specific concept statements and the muscle goes from weak to strong, that is a positive test and that supplement is indicated. Suppose someone presents with muscle spasms in the calf. I would start with instructing the client to do calf muscle stretching and then I would repeat the muscle test. If the muscle test remains weak, I touch the calf and test the concept whether calcium and magnesium supplements are indicated. If the muscle tests strong, this means that the mineral supplements are indicated.   I do another therapy localization of the calf without the supplements. If the muscle test is weak again, I investigate what else is going on. The first place I look is for dysfunction in other muscles. Muscles work together like links in a chain, so dysfunction is rarely caused by a single muscle. I repeat the muscle testing procedure of therapy localizing (identifying the problem area), determine treatment, and always follow with retesting.   If these basics are confusing, review the basics of muscle testing in Chapter 8.

Muscle balancing is another important concept. It is important to identify the keystone muscle or muscles involved in the kinetic chain. If the patient complains of muscle pain and you are not able to therapy localize, the muscle complaint is likely a compensation and is not the muscle requiring treatment.   Treating a compensation muscle is a common mistake. The first thing a doctor wants to do is either stretch or release the painful muscle. However, if this muscle is stretched out, it is not unusual for the patient to get worse and be in more pain following the therapy. The reason is simple. The muscle was too loose or weak to begin with. Think of it this way. If there are two muscles battling against each other, a strong one and a weak one, which muscle will be hurt? Put that way, most of us realize that it is the weak muscle that hurts and should not be stretched even more. Our first thought is to think that muscles are always too tight but this is not necessarily so. Muscle testing helps discern the appropriate muscles to work on. It helps determine whether you should be strengthening the muscle or if you should be stretching the muscle. Years of practice have taught me that if the painful muscle is weak, the overpowering muscle is either its antagonist or the same muscle on the opposing side. This simple secret will save your patients pain and make you look like Superhealer.

Another application for muscle testing is to evaluate whether or not allergies are an issue. First, ask the concept that allergies are an issue and then do the muscle test. If the muscle becomes weak, this is a positive test and allergies are indeed an issue. Next, identify the specific allergen. Hold the different possible allergens next to the subject's body or give a verbal suggestion naming the allergen and do the testing. When the muscle goes weak, it indicates which substance is an allergen. This is akin to clicking on a computer icon: it opens the window for you to do the work. The next step is to test the concept of the specific allergen. Start with; concept of milk, concept of wheat, concept of gluten, concept of airborne grass pollen, concept of airborne tree pollen and so on. The muscle will go weak when you identify the problematic allergen. It is wise to also test for the concept of toxins because they are different from allergens. Allergens create an immune response whereas toxins are just toxic to the body. Toxins include pesticides, herbicides, toxins given off by bacteria, chemicals, household cleaning supplies and many others.

The next progression in muscle testing is to ask more complex questions. These include highest and best and acceptable or tolerable questions. There are many applications for this line of questioning. Highest and best indicates that when all is said and done, the experience will be in the best interest of the subject. However, what the soul considers to be the highest and best interest may not agree with the ego. The primary directive of the soul consciousness is to live life with less fear and to bring more kindness into relationships and the world. This is the life path that is in the highest and best and although it may not be a smooth ride, the client will always benefit more from the altruistic consciousness rather than by the ego driven conscious mind.

"Tolerable or acceptable" questions are used to determine something that might not be great in the long run but neither will it be too harmful. For example, I reluctantly agreed to allow my son to play computer games. As he has gotten older, the games that interest him have become more violent. So, we made a deal. If I allowed him to buy the gaming equipment, then the games have to pass the muscle test. He brings a stack of games he is interested in, and we test them, right in the store. I take a game, put it in his energetic field by holding it close to his body, and say, "Test the concept that this game is in your highest and best interest." If the muscle goes weak, then that is a positive test. If the muscle stays strong, my next statement is, "Test the concept that this game is tolerable." Over the years, I have had to weaken to this position of tolerable since there are very few, if any, video games that are in anyone's highest and best interest. Allowing tolerable games is my default. This happens when we really want an experience that may not be in our highest and best interest, but it is tolerable. The experience will either have little effect or the effects will not be strongly negative. It is tolerable to have a lobster dinner, a big piece of chocolate cake and a few too many glasses of wine as long as it is not done regularly. If the concept does not test as tolerable, then one needs to be careful of consequences. These include drinking and driving, or elevated cholesterol leading to cardiac disease or heart attack. Soul consciousness knows of these probabilities. For example, I had a patient suffering from a unique musculoskeletal problem. She had made an appointment with a chiropractor who used a specific treatment technique. She asked me to muscle test whether or not she should go to this appointment. The answer was no. I asked if this was the right technique and the answer was yes. I asked if this was the right doctor to treat and the answer was yes. I told this patient that I did not understand why she should not go to her appointment if this was the right doctor and the right technique. The choice was ultimately up to her. She canceled the appointment. On the day and time of her cancelled appointment, a car went out of control in the parking lot and crashed into the waiting room of this doctor's office. After this event, we muscle tested again if she should make an appointment with this doctor. The answer was yes. It was then that I realized that the soul consciousness, in all likelihood, was aware of how the future could unfold.

Since then I have asked questions to help clarify future probabilities. I now realize that these are just probabilities and not fixed in stone. Some probabilities are set firmer than others. It depends upon whether the experience or outcome is needed by that person or perhaps humanity.

When asking questions about the future, the most important thing to do is to ask if it is okay. If the answer is no, stop. If the answer is yes, keep in mind that what you find may still be just a probability. When doing emotional work, running through probabilities and harmonizing the situation may be as good as experiencing the event.

There are other wonderful applications for using highest and best, and tolerable or acceptable questioning. You can ask questions about life decisions, trips, business adventures, and upcoming actions that are being considered. Muscle testing is a strong ally that confirms what the soul already knows. The E3 technique was created in part as a bridge between the conscious mind and the wisdom within. As with all things in life, there is a balance between logic and intuition or feelings. It is my fervent hope that the more we follow our inner wisdom, the stronger our reliance on this still, small voice becomes.

Chapter 10

THE CHARTS OF E3

THE E3 CHARTS WILL EXPLAIN the E3 process and give you the step by step tools you need to navigate this technique. .

The first chart is the Emotional Chart. Look at the man with the colored orbs down the center of his body. We will call him E3 Man. As previously mentioned in the beginning of Chapter 3, the foundation of the personality typing of E3 is based on the correlations that aura seers drew between the colors they saw and the person's personalities. I have expanded this understanding from my clinical studies and correlations with other classic personality types. These orbs on the chart represent the traditional colors and placement of the seven chakra system.

The right side of the chart lists the emotional issues and archetypes that resonate strongly with the personality that creates that color. Each color represents a chakra that pertains to a certain section of the body.

©2011 W. Mehring

Chakras and Their Emotions

Brain (General) B
Pineal (Posterior) P
Pituitary p
Testability pt T
Brain laterality or block
Governing Vessel pt GV
Collecting Vessel pt CV

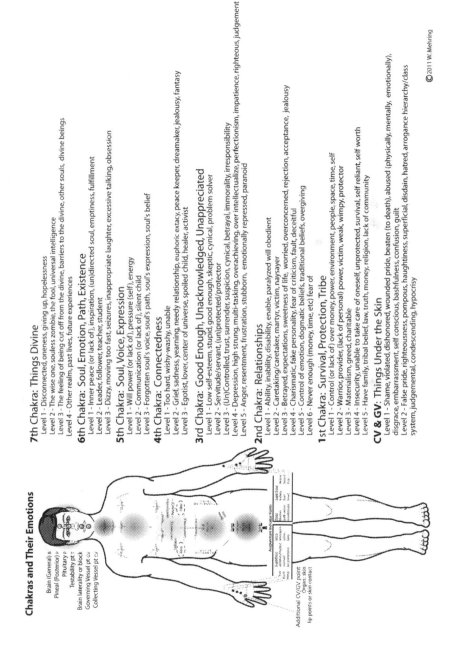

Additional CV/GV point
Organs: skin
lip points or skin contact

Acupuncture Indicator Points

7th Chakra: Things Divine
Level 1 - Disconnected, oneness, giving up, hopelessness
Level 2 - The wise one, souless zombie, the fool, universal intelligence
Level 3 - The feeling of being cut off from the divine, barriers to the divine, other souls, divine beings
Level 4 - Other realm, past lives, future experiences

6th Chakra: Soul, Emotion, Path, Existence
Level 1 - Inner peace (or lack of), inspiration, (un)directed soul, emptiness, fulfillment
Level 2 - Leader, follower, teacher, student
Level 3 - Dizzy, moving too fast, seizures, inappropriate laughter, excessive talking, obsession

5th Chakra: Soul, Voice, Expression
Level 1 - Will power (or lack of), pressure (self), energy
Level 2 - Communication (or lack of), silent child
Level 3 - Forgotten soul's voice, soul's path, soul's expression, soul's belief

4th Chakra: Connectedness
Level 1 - Too hard, wishy-washy, unable
Level 2 - Grief, sadness, yearning, needy relationship, euphoric extacy, peace keeper, dreamaker, jealousy, fantasy
Level 3 - Egotist, lover, center of universe, spoiled child, healer, activist

3rdChakra: Good Enough, Unacknowledged, Unappreciated
Level 1 - Low self-esteem, stupid, good enough, skeptic, cynical, problem solver
Level 2 - Servitude/servant, (un)protected/protector
Level 3 - (Un)Controlled, trust, surrender, suspicion, cynical, betrayal, immorality, irresponsibility
Level 4 - Depression, high strung, multi-tasking, overachieving, over intellectualize, perfectionism, impatience, righteous, judgement
Level 5 - Anger, resentment, frustration, stubborn, emotionally repressed, paranoid

2nd Chakra: Relationships
Level 1 - Ability, inability, disability, enable, paralyzed will obedient
Level 2 - Caretaking/caretaker, martyr, victim, naysayer
Level 3 - Betrayed, expectations, sweetness of life, worried, overconcerned, rejection, acceptance, jealousy
Level 4 - Charismatic, fake personality, fear of criticism, fault, deceitful
Level 5 - Control of emotion, dogmatic beliefs, traditional beliefs, overgiving
Level 6 - Never enough (money, time, etc) fear of

1st Chakra: Survival, Protection, Tribe
Level 1 - Control (or lack of) over money, power, environment, people, space, time, self
Level 2 - Warrior, provider, (lack of personal) power, victim, weak, wimpy, protector
Level 3 - Materialism, greed, charitable
Level 4 - Insecurity, unable to take care of oneself, unprotected, survival, self reliant, self worth
Level 5 - Have family, tribal belief, law, truth, money, religion, lack of community

CV & GV: Things Under the Skin
Level 1 - Shame, violated, dishonored, wounded pride, beaten (to death), abused (physically, mentally, emotionally), disgrace, embarrassment, self conscious, bashfulness, confusion, guilt
Level 2 - False pride, righteousness, pompous, haughtiness, superficial, disdain, hatred, arrogance hierarchy/class system, judgemental, condescending, hypocrisy

Dr. William D. Mehring

Ethereal Chakra 8~15 / Physical Body Chakra 1~7

7th Chakra: Bright, Multi-White
Organ - higher brain, pineal gland
Physical Level - crown of head
Neurological Level - general input

6th Chakra: Purple to Magenta
Organs - brain-general, limbic system, hypothalmus, pituitary
Physical Level - below skull cap ~C3
Neurological Level - head, 5 cm, trapezius, (paral) sympathetic

5th Chakra: Blue
Organs - thyroid, baroreceptor, carotid
Physical Level - C4~T2
Neurological Level - neck, arms

4th Chakra: Green
Organs - thymus, heart, lungs, upper stomach
Physical Level - T3~T10
Neurological Level - chest

3rd Chakra: Yellow
Organs - liver, spleen, kidney*, adrenals, upper pancreas, lower stomach
Physical Level - T10~L1, solarplexes, upper abdomen
Neurological Level - sensory to lower chest, anterior abdomen

2nd Chakra: Orange
Organs - small & large intestine, lower pancreas, upper uterus, prostate, bladder
Physical Level - L2~L5
Neurological Level - motor to lumbar, sacro/pelvis and lower extremities.
Sensory anterior & lateral lower extremities

1st Chakra: Red
Organs - sigmoid colon, testicles, lower uterus
Physical Level - sacrum, pelvis, aspects of lower extremities
Neurological Level - sensory posterior aspect of lower extremity & medial buttock, some motor to foot.

Discovery of Other Emotional Perspectives
1) Antagonistic muscle
2) Contralateral muscle
3) Opposing side of chakra

*Kidneys retain energetic connection from 4th to 2nd chakras (embryological).
*Each joint can access other chakras.
*All archetypes or roles can be accompanied with an additional emotional dynamic.

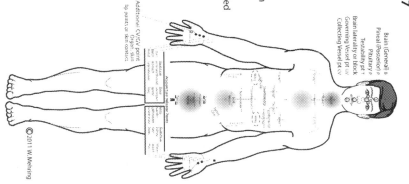

Brain (General) is
Pineal (Posterior) »
Pituitary »
Testality pt ↑
Brain laterality or block
Governing Vessel pt cv
Collecting Vessel pt cv

Additional CV/GV point
Organ: skin
tip points as skin contact

© 2011 W. Mehring

134

The next chart, the Physical and Ethereal Chakra chart, shows the relationship between specific organs and the chakras. The chakra is like a funnel. You can test all the organs and tissues of the body in that zone by just testing the chakra. This is a very efficient system.

One of the muscle testing questions asked is, "Is there anything that needs to be addressed physically?" If this is the case, you will use muscle testing to screen the various organs. There are two methods to test each of the organs. One method is to touch the reflex points that correlate with organs which are also shown on the E3 Man. To use these, simply test the arm strength looking for weakness, while touching the reflex point that corresponds to the organ. It is important to focus on the organ that you're testing. If your thoughts jump ahead to the next organ, your results will be hard to interpret.

The second method is to simply say the name of the organ. For example, say "Concept of the lung" and then muscle test. If you are therapy localizing through each of the chakras, there may be several organs to test. If you run through all the organs that are listed on the left side of the chart, do not forget to test the musculoskeletal system and connective tissue in that area. If you still come up blank, you may need to be more specific.

Talking with the innate using the E3 protocol will tell you what else needs attention. The E3 protocol addresses the need for nutrients, homeopathy or other treatments. Once you have resolved any physical requirements, it is important to go back and check for an emotional component. It is quite common for there to be a latent emotional issue that will not show up until the physical issue is resolved. If there had been nothing to address physically, the next step would have been to look at the emotional components. Remember, most physical ailments have an emotional component at the root, or as compensation to the area in stress.

The main foundation of the E3 process is emotional work. We return to the chart showing the chakras and their emotions.

135

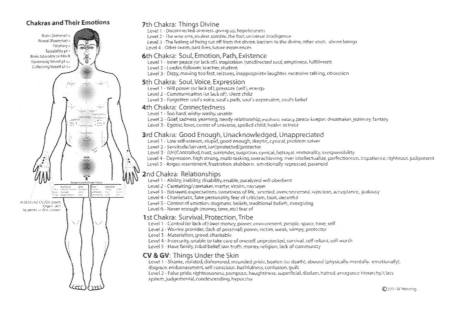

Chakras and Their Emotions

Brain (Sternness) >
Pineal (Posterior) >
Pituitary >
Testability pt >
Brain Intensity or block
(Sensing Vessel pt w
Collecting Vessel pt c/

Additional CV/GV point
(organ site)
(ю points on skin) shown)

7th Chakra: Things Divine
Level 1 - Disconnected, oneness, giving up, hopelessness
Level 2 - The wise one, souless zombie, the fool, universal intelligence
Level 3 - The feeling of being cut off from the divine, barriers to the divine, other souls, divine beings
Level 4 - Other realm, past lives, future experiences

6th Chakra: Soul, Emotion, Path, Existence
Level 1 - Inner peace (or lack of), inspiration, (un)directed soul, emptiness, fulfillment
Level 2 - Leader, follower, teacher, student
Level 3 - Dizzy, moving too fast, seizures, inappropriate laughter, excessive talking, obsession

5th Chakra: Soul, Voice, Expression
Level 1 - Will power (or lack of), pressure (self), energy
Level 2 - Communication (or lack of), silent child
Level 3 - Forgotten soul's voice, soul's path, soul's expression, soul's belief

4th Chakra: Connectedness
Level 1 - Too hard, wishy-washy, unable
Level 2 - Grief, sadness, yearning, needy relationship, euphoric extacy, peace keeper, dreamaker, jealousy, fantasy
Level 3 - Egotist, lover, center of universe, spoiled child, healer, activist

3rd Chakra: Good Enough, Unacknowledged, Unappreciated
Level 1 - Low self-esteem, stupid, good enough, skeptic, cynical, problem solver
Level 2 - Servitude/servant, (un)protected/protector
Level 3 - (Un)Controlled, trust, surrender, suspicion, cynical, betrayal, immorality, irresponsibility
Level 4 - Depression, high strung, multi-tasking, overachieving, over intellectualize, perfectionism, impatience, righteous, judgement
Level 5 - Anger, resentment, frustration, stubborn, emotionally repressed, paranoid

2nd Chakra: Relationships
Level 1 - Ability, inability, disability, enable, paralyzed will obedient
Level 2 - Caretaking/caretaker, martyr, victim, naysayer
Level 3 - Betrayed, expectations, sweetness of life, worried, overconcerned, rejection, acceptance, jealousy
Level 4 - Charismatic, fake personality, fear of criticism, fault, deceitful
Level 5 - Control of emotion, dogmatic, beliefs, traditional beliefs, overgiving
Level 6 - Never enough (money, time, etc) fear of

1st Chakra: Survival, Protection, Tribe
Level 1 - Control (or lack of) over money, power, environment, people, space, time, self
Level 2 - Warrior, provider, (lack of personal) power, victim, weak, wimpy, protector
Level 3 - Materialism, greed, charitable
Level 4 - Insecurity, unable to take care of oneself, unprotected, survival, self reliant, self worth
Level 5 - Have family, tribal belief, law, truth, money, religion, lack of community

CV & GV: Things Under the Skin
Level 1 - Shame, violated, dishonored, wounded pride, beaten (to death), abused (physically, mentally, emotionally), disgrace, embarrassment, self conscious, bashfulness, confusion, guilt
Level 2 - False pride, righteousness, pompous, haughtiness, superficial, disdain, hatred, arrogance hierarchy/class system, judgemental, condescending, hypocrisy

©2011 W. Mehring

The heading represents the chakra number. The chakra colors are listed in the headings. The levels listed below the chakra headings divide the different emotional dynamics into their emotional families. Each of the chakras has a level that lists the negative and positive archetypes. The lines next to the levels are the chakra issues as well as some of the main issues of that personality color. *This does not mean that each personality is limited to the emotion in their color category.* Far from it. While each of us can experience any emotional issue, we see it through our personality filter. However, there is a much greater probability that a person's issues correlate with their color, more than any other color. Remember that each of us has a different ratio of all of the personalities. No one is strictly one color. The dominant color wins in most decisions, beliefs and actions. We generally have a primary personality and a secondary personality that balances the primary or is needed in certain situations. The personality that we have strongly indicates life lessons that need to be harmonized. Secondary personalities can also be protective mechanisms.

Recall that throughout our life we learn to integrate the aspects of other personalities to achieve balance and to overcome our primary personality's greatest chaos. If you take the personality test and find that you are completely missing one personality color, chances are you surround yourself with people with this personality. The reason is to learn, appreciate, and speak their language.

Let's review the emotional issues, themes and archetypes of the four basic personalities. You may want to study the personality descriptions in Chapter 3 to deepen your understanding. This is an important component in assisting clients. Use the personality test or muscle testing to ascertain their primary and secondary personality colors. Though you'll use this information to guide the sessions, ask questions that reveal the client's personality as well as their main issues.

1ST CHAKRA: RED

Let's start with the first chakra or the Red personality. This personality works on the ability to survive, protect and create connection and loyalty within their tribe. Think of the tribe as a metaphor for family, place of worship, the fellow warriors with whom they go to battle, their company or collections of people with similar ideology. They are always fortifying, unifying or expanding their tribes. They do not like to show weakness to people outside of their tribe.

The Warrior is the most common Red archetype. Reds quickly learn about power and control in work as well as play. They are also the first people to help when work needs to be done. Reds do not waste time. They believe in hard work and dislike a lot of drama. They enjoy battling or watching sports battles. Reds establish organizations and companies so they can be in charge of them. They understand the strategies of money, materialism, superior physicality, hierarchy, unified beliefs and strength. They believe in things as black-and-white, as well as literal translations and one truth.

Reds thrive as bankers, financial managers, soldiers, military strategists and officers, policemen, firefighters, and sports coaches as well as players. They are also found in the hierarchy of the world's religions. These roles represent obtaining control, enforcing the concepts of right and wrong, gaining power through strength and conflict, and acquisition of money. Reds are motivated by the fear of being vulnerable, powerless or broke. Red issues revolve around losing control and power over people, places and things. They will struggle with the weaknesses they perceive in themselves, their ideology and the archetype of being a victim.

Reds need to be aware of the things they want power over, as well as how they want others to conform to their beliefs and ideologies. These issues highlight the opportunities for Reds to confront their fears of not having enough control, power, strength, or their fear of people with differing beliefs. Not every Red desires uniformity of belief, however, there is more intolerance in the Red personality than others. When they are done harmonizing their life issues, they are some of the finest examples of generosity, fairness, and humility.

2ND CHAKRA: ORANGE PERSONALITY

The second chakra, represented by the Orange personality, works a lot on relationships. This personality can be characterized as very sweet, kind and thoughtful. They can also be very entertaining. The underlying Orange action is the need to be liked. They want this so much that they will sacrifice their own self.

The archetype is the Caretaker. The negative and opposite archetype is the Martyr. Oranges create and solidify their relationships by taking care of others. They are extremely good at anticipating the other's needs as well as having a sense about their character. Unfortunately, fully embodying this archetype means they are doing too much for everyone else. The unspoken contract is reciprocal friendship, loyalty, or caretaking exchanged with the other person. Caretakers habitually sublimate themselves for others and believe that they are selflessly giving, but this soon breeds resentment. As the Orange Caretaker shifts into resentment, they embody the Martyr.

The Martyr is someone who sacrifices themselves for a person or cause. However, the reality is that they do everything for their own needs. They search for people to appreciate them, think highly of them and hope that others support or care for them. The emotional issues that go along with this are betrayal, false expectations and over giving. The issue with over giving is that Oranges take on the traits, beliefs and actions that others want. This makes it hard for them to become themselves.

Oranges need to work on self-acceptance and realizing that they are good enough. They need to walk into their fear and tell people exactly how they feel and what they want. Oranges dread others not liking or admiring them; however, they must express their opinions so people see exactly who they are. They must come out of the cave. After harmonizing, Oranges do not have to pretend around their friends. This relieves and restores energy. They will need help as they lose surface friendships and find deeper, more meaningful relationships with people who really appreciate their true character.

3RD CHAKRA: YELLOW

The 3rd chakra represented by the color Yellow is the area that reflects the universal struggle to feel good enough. This is a lifelong struggle for the Yellow personality. Yellows strive for self-reliance and self-improvement. However, once Yellow reaches a goal, they immediately set the bar higher. They are very inventive regarding the most efficient route to excellence. Yellows don't mind doing things by themselves because they are self-actuated and value themselves as self-made.

This leads to several central issues for the Yellow personality. They must learn how to value process over product, enjoy attaining a goal, and be mindful and present. Yellows can be self- righteous because of the high moral compass they choose to live by. One of their greatest frustrations is that the rest of the world does not share their sense of morality. To Yellows, everything would be great if the world wised up and did what was right. Yellows make it their job to bring about social changes as they are very principled and ideological.

Yellows have a lifelong journey of finding balance between feelings and logic . To find happiness, they must integrate their feelings. Anger, resentment, frustration, stubbornness, paranoia, and skepticism are listed as 3rd chakra emotional issues. These words have a real zing to them. When a Yellow person is having a dark day, watch out: they can launch a verbal barrage of sizzling projectiles. Misleading and manipulating others are early weapons of choice if their internal chaos and frustration become overpowering. The Yellow ego can be satiated by controlling others because making someone more miserable than themselves means they've achieved a higher status. The negative archetypes include being a Servant, the Slow Student, and Anarchist.

Yellows need assistance coming down off their high horse. They need to learn how to function in an imperfect world. Issues of hierarchy and being judgmental are at the top of the list of things to work on.

4ᵗʰ CHAKRA: GREEN

The 4th chakra is the home of the Green personality. The buzzword here is connection. Their issues all have to do with being connected, wanting to be connected or feeling disconnected. Protection, relationship, and good enough indicate what Greens want and work towards, but for appearances sake. Greens fear disconnection and they create and feel chaos because they try too hard to connect.

Greens possess an amazing knack to emote unconditional love. They are soothed by being touched, touching others either physically or emotionally and embody the sensuous archetype of the Lover. They are also passionate, empathic, and intuitive and root for the underdog.

The word "freedom" is hardwired into green's makeup which leads to planetary, environmental and human activism. Greens wear lots of tie-dyed, colorful accessories with bumper stickers that say things like "Free Tibet" and "Save the Whales." Greens detest limits so they try to control their personal space before anyone else can. When Greens combine their extroverted nature with their passion, they make good leaders.

On the negative side, Greens can be bossy and stubborn. Negative archetypes include being center of the universe and the Egotist. The Green personality is dramatic and requires more attention from others. When not feeling loved or connected, they demand everything to revolve around their needs. It is the Green's misfortune to feel they must attain super status in whatever they do. Without super status they do not trust the connection and risk falling apart. They require others to admire, fall in love with, befriend, or smile at them. Feeling disconnected brings up issues of grief, sadness, yearning, needy relationships, abandonment, and despair.

Ecstasy relates to being connected; however, the emotional characteristics of head in the clouds, loftiness, overgiving, over sympathizing, wishy-washiness, obsessing, drama, and nervousness relate more to the nature of the personality. Luckily they typically are super energetic. Greens wake up excited about life and the search for more connections.

It is important to note that some personalities can look and act similarly. This is the case with the Green and Red personalities because the Red personality is also gregarious by nature. Greens and Reds seek connection in order to build their tribe. The difference is in their ideologies, which actually makes them opposing forces. Reds believe in tradition, uniformity, literal interpretations, one truth and the proven methods. Reds are logical and don't like anything that is beyond their five senses. Greens are the polar opposite. They believe in unconventional ideas, diversity, gray interpretations, many ideologies, and quickly become bored of repetition. Greens are instinctual and speak of things that go beyond the five senses. Greens support the planet and humanity in general, while reds support political and religious affiliations.

Again, all of the above trends describe personalities early in the harmonization process. While none of us likes to see ourselves early on in the process, with honesty and effort, we can look very different at the end of the road.

5ᵀᴴ CHAKRA: BLUE

The region around the throat or the 5th chakra is usually seen as blue. The 5th, 6th and 7th chakras do not have as much to do with the basic 4 personalities but more to do with the person's interaction with the consciousness of the soul. Extroverts show more blue in their aura. Issues found here indicate lost connection to either their own voice, or their creative expression. However, the most common emotional issue is a lost connection to what the soul wants to say to them or through them. The opposing archetypes are the Communicator and Silent Child.

6ᵀᴴ CHAKRA: PURPLE

The 6th chakra is commonly seen as purple or magenta and is located around the head, including the brain. This chakra deals with existence, emotions, and also the soul's path. A lot of purple either means clients are strongly connected to the soul or that they are tuned in to their feelings or intuition. Seeing more purple in the aura is the domain of the introvert. The opposing archetypes are Leader versus the Follower, and Teacher versus

Student. The Green personality and the 6th chakra are strongly related. Because Greens are intuitive and have a strong desire to connect to the soul's emotions, they will have issues in this chakra. Level 3 of this chakra lists many Green personality traits and behaviors, but these can be felt by anyone. Level 1 depicts a state of being relating to the soul's status, as well as one's own status.

7ᵀᴴ CHAKRA: ALL COLORS

The 7th chakra is commonly referred to as the gate to the upper world and is thought of as our connecting place to Divine universal consciousness. As with the Divine, it has the aspects of all colors and is in a constant state of change. Level 2 deals with the opposing archetypes of the Wise One or universal intelligence versus the Fool or the Zombie. Level 4 gives another way to access things of the divine realm.

The idea is that when we remove the barriers and emotional issues separating us from this universal conscious intelligence, we are the Wise One. When we are disconnected from our soul we lack inner direction and become zombie-like. The Zombie is easily led by fear due to lack of soul connection. This was portrayed in the story about the Ba'al Shem Tov.

Level 1 lists the emotions associated with separation from this concept of a divine realm. Level 3 articulates things that people feel cut off from in the divine realms. When your client discovers these terms, ask what these terms mean to them. This will give you direction. Most people have unique interpretations of 7ᵗʰ chakra expressions. The 7ᵗʰ chakra emanates from the top of the head. It is best accessed by placing the hand above the head with the palm facing down.

The final list of emotions is found in the lower right, titled "CV & GV: Things Under the Skin." CV &GV stands for conception vessel and governing vessel. This is where the acupuncture meridian systems all connect. Governing vessel and conception vessel points are very familiar to acupuncturists and energy workers. These are great points to connect to a multiple meridian source to see if there is something that needs to be addressed. The meridians run over the skin and are intricately enmeshed with the skin. The two levels of CV and GV have to do with living in a world of judgment. This is where shame, blame, embarrassment, self-consciousness, arrogance, hatred, hierarchy, class systems, dishonor, and guilt live. You will notice patterns in certain personalities that use these qualities to make themselves feel better, as well as to coerce themselves towards a more rigid and righteous path. The words on both lists are very judgmental in nature. When these words are spoken, they inflict us with harmful neurochemicals.

The opposite of someone who employs CV and GV, a judgmental and self-righteous life, is someone who is connected to their inner wisdom and navigates life with a strong moral compass. Their actions are self-evident and self-actuated. They do not have conflict over the right direction. These individuals are whole so they do not need to chase. Their ego no longer strives to put other people down or lift themselves up to feel good enough. It is important to realize that when people use the language of judgment, shame, blame and guilt, they did not get what was needed during the formative years. The primary archetypes are the Victim, Martyr, Servant and Follower.

Our society teaches two main methods to change and correct our path. One is to tear ourselves down to a point that we are so angry that we decide to do better. This is the "what doesn't kill you makes you stronger" school of thought and is common for the masculine personalities, Red and Yellow. The problem with this way of thinking is that the underlying principle screams "you are worthless." Despite years of constantly trying to prove yourself, and overcoming odds, at the roots are the beliefs "you are not good enough," "you lack something," "you are not whole," and "you are bad to the bone." The internal question is, "When will someone learn the awful truth about me?" It takes a lot of energy to keep these beliefs hidden.

The other path to growth is discovering our wholeness. This entails removing all damage caused by self-deprecating terms such as embarrassment, shame and guilt found in the CV/GV category. You will need to instruct your clients to remove all of this language, or to notice when they sound like a Victim or a Martyr and then find the emotional event where they first lost their sense of wholeness and remove the filters. When clients use this method, they don't need to *make* themselves act differently because change comes naturally. This work cannot be completed in one session but it is very important work. Wholeness reveals Oneness.

Another section on the Ethereal Chakra chart is titled Discovery of Other Emotional Perspectives. The last line of this section reads: *All*

archetypes or roles can be accompanied with an additional emotional dynamic.
If you are working with someone and an archetype comes up, it is important
that you understand all of the archetypes characteristics. Search for how
the client embodies these features. If the archetype is brought up, there is
something dysfunctional about it in the client's life. Usually this applies to
the negative archetypes such as Victim or Martyr. Positive archetypes can
also be out of balance. Imagine if a Lover, Protector or Warrior has gone too
far. Out of balance archetypal behaviors create their own set of problems.

You want to make the client aware of how the archetype manifests in
their life, and then transform the archetype to its positive archetype by
harmonizing their beliefs. If a positive archetype comes up, then it means
it is out of balance and the person is trying to become more like that
archetype. It is your job to find out what blocks them from embodying what
they wish to become. Once you discover how they are wrestling with the
archetype, test the idea that there is an accompanying emotional dynamic
to this archetype. In fact, there are usually several dynamics. When you get
done with the first issue, investigate further by testing the idea of another
emotional component. This shatters the negative archetypes.

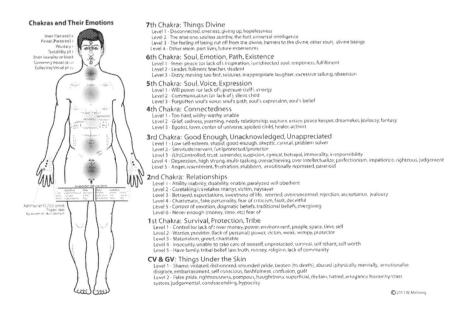

Chakras and Their Emotions

7th Chakra: Things Divine
Level 1 - Disconnected, oneness, giving up, hopelessness
Level 2 - The wise one, souless zombie, the fool, universal intelligence
Level 3 - The feeling of being cut off from the divine, barriers to the divine, other souls, divine beings
Level 4 - Other realm, past lives, future experiences

6th Chakra: Soul, Emotion, Path, Existence
Level 1 - Inner peace (or lack of), inspiration, (un)directed soul, emptiness, fulfillment
Level 2 - Leader, follower, teacher, student
Level 3 - Dizzy, moving too fast, seizures, inappropriate laughter, excessive talking, obsession

5th Chakra: Soul, Voice, Expression
Level 1 - Will power (or lack of), pressure (self), energy
Level 2 - Communication (or lack of), silent child
Level 3 - Forgotten soul's voice, soul's path, soul's expression, soul's belief

4th Chakra: Connectedness
Level 1 - Too hard, wishy-washy, unable
Level 2 - Grief, sadness, yearning, needy relationship, euphoric extacy, peace keeper, dreamaker, jealousy, fantasy
Level 3 - Egotist, lover, center of universe, spoiled child, healer, activist

3rd Chakra: Good Enough, Unacknowledged, Unappreciated
Level 1 - Low self-esteem, stupid, good enough, skeptic, cynical, problem solver
Level 2 - Servitude/servant, (un)protected/protector
Level 3 - (Un)Controlled, trust, surrender, suspicion, cynical, betrayal, immorality, irresponsibility
Level 4 - Depression, high strung, multi tasking, overachieving, over intellectualize, perfectionism, impatience, righteous, judgement
Level 5 - Anger, resentment, frustration, stubborn, emotionally repressed, paranoid

2nd Chakra: Relationships
Level 1 - Ability, inability, disability, enable, paralyzed will obedient
Level 2 - Caretaking/caretaker, martyr, victim, naysayer
Level 3 - Betrayed, expectations, sweetness of life, worried, overconcerned, rejection, acceptance, jealousy
Level 4 - Charismatic, fake personality, fear of criticism, fault, deceitful
Level 5 - Control of emotion, dogmatic beliefs, traditional beliefs, overgiving
Level 6 - Never enough (money, time, etc) fear of

1st Chakra: Survival, Protection, Tribe
Level 1 - Control (or lack of) over money, power, environment, people, space, time, self
Level 2 - Warrior, provider, (lack of personal) power, victim, weak, wimpy, protector
Level 3 - Materialism, greed, charitable
Level 4 - Insecurity, unable to take care of oneself, unprotected, survival, self reliant, self worth
Level 5 - Have family, tribal belief, law, truth, money, religion, lack of community

CV & GV: Things Under the Skin
Level 1 - Shame, violated, dishonored, wounded pride, beaten (to death), abused (physically, mentally, emotionally), disgrace, embarrassment, self conscious, bashfulness, confusion, guilt
Level 2 - False pride, righteousness, pompous, haughtiness, superficial, disdain, hatred, arrogance, hierarchy/class system, judgemental, condescending, hypocrisy

© 2011 W. Mehring

When we examine the Emotional Chakra chart once again, we can see there are a few other miscellaneous treasures on the chart that may be valuable to you.

The circled letters on E3 Man's face represent different structures on the head with explanations of these structures found to the left. These points may need to be examined. To be more specific, simply point your fingers at the area where that portion of the brain exists, have the client visualize that structure in their head, and test the concept that the issue is with the cerebral cortex, the limbic center or wherever structure you are investigating. Note that the pineal gland is accessed from the back of the head. The pituitary is accessed by placing two fingers on each side of the upper bridge of the nose. This polarity point is found between the highest point of the nose and the lowest part of the forehead.

There is a dotted line through the middle of the E3 Man's face. This helps test for blockage between the brain's two hemispheres, what is called brain laterality. This can be a therapeutic point to assess whether or not a person lacks balance between the right and left side of their brains or masculine versus feminine. This also helps people who have a hard time holding onto memories, which occurs if the experiences cannot cross-lateralize from one side of the brain to the other. This is also a great point to check when working with somebody with learning disabilities.

Another chart item is titled wrist pulse points. There are superficial and deep wrist points which correlate to different organs as well as the five elements of acupuncture, Fire, Earth, Metal, Water and Wood. Use these points to scan through the organs quickly. First test the superficial points. This is done by gently resting three fingers on these three points on one wrist simultaneously and then testing for positive therapy localization. If the arm goes weak, then test each pulse point individually until you find which caused the positive test. If the superficial points did not test positive, then press down on those points a little more to access the organs deep reflex points. If the deep wrist points do not therapy localize, move to the opposite wrist and begin with the superficial points, followed by the deep points.

There is another section on the chart called "Discovery of Other Emotional Perspectives". This is best used for musculoskeletal problems when you want to access many perspectives about a central issue. If someone has a chronic muscle injury that won't heal, it is usually because there is an unresolved emotional issue inhibiting the area's natural healing ability. In other words, the chi or life force is stuck.

Imagine that the client has a left bicep tendonitis or strain. Therapy localization to the bicep yields a positive result. You test the idea of an emotional issue and again get a positive result. You refer to the chart, test and determine that the issue is abandonment. You harmonized that experience and now want to get a better grasp of all the layers that exist around this person's abandonment. You will next test the antagonist to the bicep, which is the tricep (Antagonist is #1 under the Discovery of Other Emotional Persepctives heading). The issue found in the tricep could be betrayal. Once that is harmonized, therapy localize to the bicep on the opposite side. This gives you another perspective. The emotion might be grief with a completely different time frame that supports the issue constellation of abandonment. You might even go as far as testing the tricep on the opposite side as well. This is a great way to understand and deconstruct the constellation of this family of issues .

Another revealing E3 technique is using the opposing or posterior side of the chakra. Most of our work is done while facing the patient. This means we are accessing the emotional issues from the front of the person. Once you develop a good sense of trust with the client, therapy localize to the same chakra, but from the back. If you have a positive therapy localization test, the next concept to test is a shadow component. This test will differentiate between the shadow issue and another issue that is residing in the same chakra. Understand that the shadow issue is a very deep and tender one. It is the issue that the person has hidden from public view for a very long time. These issues will not be revealed until you have developed trust. They are extremely valuable in unlocking issues that come up session after session. They can represent the core or the armoring that sustains an individual's belief system.

One final heading on the chart is titled Ethereal Chakras 8-15. This is to suggest that there are additional energy centers not located on the body; energetic emanations that go out beyond our physical self. There are many mystical writings from different traditions that support this belief. You can place your hand in different areas around the body, especially above the head, and just to the side of the head and body, and try therapy localizing. What you find may surprise you. If the emotional issues or archetypes are not on the list, ask intuitively for a picture that can help the person. If this work interests you, I recommend studying Jewish mysticism called Kabbalah. The diagrams for the Tree of Life show ten sephirot, or emanations to exist outside of the body. The information gleaned from these centers is more ethereal but can be therapy localized. Most clients may not relate to this type of therapy localization; however, there will also be people that love this sort of work. Try the technique with another muscle testing practitioner or one of your Green friends and see what happens. As practitioners, we must expand our concepts.

This concludes the Emotional and Ethereal charts. Now we move on to the detailed work of the E3 process.

(A) BACKGROUND

Ask religious beliefs, issues of past lives, etc.
- Working within their framework

How muscle tests work. A change of strength.
- Conscious mind/Physical dimension
- Sub/Super conscious mind/Soul dimension

How organs, chakras, or other parts of the body
- Hold and process emotional issues.

Cocreate and discuss the mystical journey
- With the emotional dynamic
- With the players in the story of your life

Initiation of the Mystical Journey
- Specific sensitizing event to your chosen journey
- We must cross a line to learn
- Time ribbon of experiences
- Recreation of self through free choice
- Steps of evolution

(B) OPENING

---- Clear yourself, open & connect
---- Ask permission to begin working together;
---- Testability muscle test. 1) show them their strong, 2) show them their weak

Treatment Possibilities	Places of Pain	Chakra (7 - 0?)	Aura (Template?)	Intuitive Pulse	Organ	(OTHER)*
Emotional facilitation		○	○	○	○	○
Energetic facilitation		○	○	○	○	○
Vibrational/Sound facilitation		○	○	○	○	○
Vibrational substances Homeopathic, Bach, aroma therapeutic, etc.		○	○	○	○	○
Nutritional fortification Vitamins, foods, supplements, etc.		○	○	○	○	○
Physical Medicine		○	○	○	○	○
Something else Ask Priority of Treatment		○	○	○	○	○
Accupuncture		○	○	○	○	○

*Includes Feelings, Situations, Dreams, Memories...sky's the limit

(C) DETERMINE THE EMOTIONAL DYNAMIC

all entry points lead to chakra emotions:

W =Weak
S =Strong
TP =Treatment Possibilities

(D) DETERMINE WHO OR WHAT IS INCLUDED IN THE PRESENT DAY STORY: "The Trigger"

Physical World	Relationships/Roles
Money	Mon.	People, and your interactions
Time	Thur	with them
Work	Wed.	Interactions or relationships
Things	Tue	with other than people
Finances	Fri	YOU and the roles you play
Planet (Sited)	Sat	Archetypes

Test/evaluate that we are dealing with the Physical World
The Physical World being M, T, W, Th, F, S.

(E) DISTILL AND COMBINE THE EMOTIONAL THEME WITH THE PLAYERS AND DISCOVER THE STORY LINE OF THE CURRENT EVENT

Can you tell me how these two might go together. Keep it simple. I feel _____ when _____ happened

(F) CREATE AN ESSENCE STATEMENT

The emotional dynamic is simply stated and the trigger is generalized so that it can travel through time and still include any possibilities of what happened earlier. Muscle test this until the essence statement is clear and open-ended.

(G) DETERMINE THE TIME LINE OF THE ORIGINAL SENSITIZING EVENT

"Let's test the idea of the earliest sensitizing event where you felt _____ when _____

(H) EXPERIENCE AND EXPAND THE ORIGINAL SENSITIZING EVENT

Expand and explore how the **Emotional Dynamic** played itself out with the **Trigger** in the original sensitizing event. (You will need to repeat D to determine the original sensitizing trigger) Use probing statements to 1) determine the extent of the emotional dynamic in the original sensitizing event; 2) determine how the plot of the present day issue connects or parallels with the original sensitizing event.

(I) EVOLVING AND EXPERIENCING EVENT

STEP 1 AWAKENING SELF-REMEMBRANCE
Allow the client to experience this initial sensitizing event. Acknowledging/Breathing/Releasing

STEP 2 SELF-REMEMBRANCE
Allow them to slowly review the dynamic of this event.

STEP 3 AWARENESS
Allow them to open up to the time ribbon that connects the many experiences in their life where the emotional dynamic has been operating. See how it has played itself out from each chakra's point of view and then experience the many layers of this belief system.

TRANSITION
Once they wish for change is current with being able to see the past behaviors, the seeds of a new dynamic are revealed.

STEP 4 TRANSFORMATION
See yourself in this situation using the principles of evolution, the strengths and experiences of this life and other infinite lives as you revisit the same situation. Allow this to unfold and evolve over and over again until new dialogue and new outcomes are created.

Ask the person to reveal how the experience unfolded. As they do, listen for incongruency with principles of evolution and/or muscle test.

The person can at any time return back to evolve the outcome and do additional work.

STEP 5
Eyes open to future probabilities
Utilizing intuitive aid and insight ask the person, "if this dynamic were to recreate itself in your future, how might it come up?"

STEP 6
Premonitory Test if it's OK to view future probabilities for the purpose of evolving. Test, if it's beneficial.

Muscle test/result that their experience is beneficial in evolving this emotional dynamic.

STEP 7
Through the mind's eye evolve through the future probability utilizing all new dynamics and tools. Make as many transformative sweeps as needed.

Ask the person to reveal how the experience unfolded. As they do, listen for incongruency with principles of evolution and/or muscle test.

This is the place of final presumptions before that dynamic manifests itself in the physical world.

STEP 8 CONFORMATION
I am well in the physical world. The person must take a step where they have never gone in the physical world. Know that this step will be difficult. It will be saddled with some of their greatest fears.

The lessons will continue to manifest until the dynamic has completely changed and there is no hesitation to take the new step.

STEP 9 INFORMATION TRANSFORMATION
A new feeling of Strength and Grace that replaces fear.

A new emotional dynamic is in place and the old situation stops manifesting.

STEP 10
Test the original emotion, original, current & future triggers and previously active probing statements.

E³
Emotional
Energetic
Evolution

© 2013 W. Mehring

THE E3 PROCESS
These ten steps are the basics of the E3 process.

A. Client and practitioner get comfortable and share their backgrounds.

B. Ask permission to begin working together, introduce muscle testing and determine treatment direction. This is referred to as Opening.

C. Determine the emotional dynamic.

D. Determine who or what is included in the story. What is the trigger?

E. Distill the emotional theme between those involved and discover the story line of the current event.

F. Create an essence statement.

G. Determine the timeline of the original sensitizing event.

H. Experience and expand the original sensitizing event.

I. Evolve and reframe the experience.

J. Test the need for future probabilities.

In the simplest of terms, you care seeking to find the emotion and how it manifests in the client's daily life. Next, determine how it started and who was involved. Finally, have the client feel and change the emotion. If it's helpful to look into the future, the door will open. Keep this simple framework in your mind as you delve into the specifics of the E3 process.

A. BACKGROUND

(A) BACKGROUND

Ask religious beliefs, issues of past lives, etc.
  -Working within their framework

How muscle tests work. A change of strength.
  -Conscious mind/Physical dimension
  -Sub/Super conscious mind/Soul dimension

How organs, chakras, or other parts of the body
  -Hold and process emotional issues.

Cocreate and discuss the mystical journey
  -With the emotional dynamic
  -With the players in the story of your life

Initiation of the Mystical Journey
  -Specific sensitizing event to your chosen journey
  -We must cross a line to learn
  -Time ribbon of experiences
  -Recreation of self through free choice
  -Steps of evolution

(B) OPENING

----Clear yourself, open & connect
----Ask permission to begin working together:
----Testability muscle test: 1) show them their strong; 2) show them their weak

Treatment Possibilities	Places of Pain	Chakra (7-00)	Aura (Templates)	Intuitive Point	Organ	(OTHER)*
Emotional facilitation	⟁	◯	◯	◯	◯	◯
Energetic facilitation	⟁	◯	◯	◯	◯	◯
Vibrational/Sound facilitation	⟁	◯	◯	◯	◯	◯
Vibrational substances Homeopathic, Bach, aroma therapeutic, etc.	⟁	◯	◯	◯	◯	◯
Nutritional fortification Vitamins, foods, supplements, etc.	⟁	◯	◯	◯	◯	◯
Physical Medicine	⟁	◯	◯	◯	◯	◯
Something else Ask Priority of Treatment	⟁	◯	◯	◯	◯	◯
Accupunture	⟁	◯	◯	◯	◯	◯

*Includes Feelings, Situations, Dreams, Memories...sky's the limit

The first step is to delve into your client's belief system, most importantly what they believe about the concepts of heaven, hell, the after- life and past life experience. It is inevitable that someone will have an issue that predates this life. It may be from an energetic realm, that some would call heaven, or a previous life. It is good to know your client's viewpoints about these issues ahead of time so that you can speak to them in language and terms they will resonate with. Your client's belief system may be very different from your own but it is vital *not to force your beliefs onto your client.* Becoming familiar with the other person's beliefs and language will honor them and make them feel more secure with the interaction. Religious ideology does not necessarily dictate whether or not they believe in past life experience. For example, I have met many Christians who believe in past lives even though a particular church may have a dogmatic position. Christianity, Islam are the only major religions that contemplate a single life.

All of the other major religions and philosophies, from Judaism to Taoism have a re-creation or reincarnation story. Ask your clients how the Creator impacts their daily life. Another valuable question is, "How do you get close to God or the Creator?" When it come to religious or spiritual beliefs, people can usually be categorized in one of two ways: those who do God's work by following the rules, and those who find God by meditating or walking in nature.

After the client shares their background, I explain the E3 process using the client's own world view as my guide, choosing any of the following terms based on their language. I explain that muscle testing is a way to access the neurological system, the subconscious mind, the innate, or the soul. I play the Flintstones name game (described in Chapter 8) to put the client at ease and to keep the process light hearted at the beginning. Clients are usually very surprised at the muscle test when they can easily feel the difference between strong and weak. This is very important as it shows them that the testing is real and that it works as a therapeutic tool. If they need more convincing, one can test question with obvious answers. For example, test the concept, "You like breathing," or test the concept, "You like eating." These will elicit a positive response and the client can understand what that feels like.

Sometimes, as part of the E3 explanation, a discussion about the mystical journey, or the journey of life is in order. I suggest books such as Journey of Souls by Dr. Michael Newton, Many Lives, Many Masters, by Dr. Brian L. Weiss, M.D., or mystical texts from Buddhism, Judaism or Taoism. These teachings indicate that we are each a unique soul, inseparable from a Creation much bigger than we can contemplate. Our consciousness or eternal soul is persistent through many lives. One of life's purposes, from the mystical point of view, is that Creation is experiencing itself through us. We are one of the many expansions of Creation. Relationships are one of the sweetest parts of this experience but there is also internal chaos, which itself is an integral part of the Creation. Part of what we are here to do in this life is to harmonize the chaos. I use the word Creation instead of God, but most people find God more familiar. Think of the Creator as a verb rather than a noun. Life is more about an active, continuous creation or re-creation that we are an integral part of. Rabbi David Cooper has even written a book titled God is a Verb: Kabbalah and the Practice of Mystical Judaism. This creation process repairs the internal chaotic brokenness of us as individuals and in turn, the world.

In this life creation, we chose a body in a specific family, with just the right personality that gives us the opportunities to activate and harmonize our main core issues. Nearly all emotional issues center on not feeling good enough, disconnection and lack of control. These issues may seem innocent but their end result is fear, anger, greed, judgment, hatred, killing, bigotry, wars, and intolerance. It is our job to transform this internal self-destruction, thereby transforming the destructive external world. Creation is trying to create a system that is self healing. Imagine that you are Creation awakening each day to turmoil and chaos. It would be like waking each morning with a stomach ache. We are a part of the team whose job is to gobble up internal chaos. Another metaphor would be comparing us to white blood cells. Each day, these cells jump on the arterial and venous freeways, searching for harmful substances. After the cells identify these elements, they neutralize them. I can imagine us doing the same thing with the Creator giving hints all along the way to help Its subparts resolve the chaos inside of it. God gives us constant positive feedback to resolve our issues and harmonize the chaos.

This process transforms life's fear filter into an eternal awe experience. The mystics teach the work of transforming oneself into a vessel of internal peace and love as in their eyes, we are all interconnected as One. By doing our own work, we help the collective consciousness, helping others just as much as we help ourselves. The more we find inner peace in our own chaos, the more all living things find peace. The more we do this work, the more we can realize and experience our connection to God, the Creator, or perhaps our true inner self. The more we do this work, the closer we come to understanding there is complete oneness in a world working together in peace. The path to inner peace is finding and accepting one's radically unique self, and connecting with our inner soul, not whether a particular story about the universal consciousness is true or not.

The harmonization process has no downside as there is lasting reward in getting rid of one's emotional baggage. Lasting reward means being able to experiencing peace in situations that once caused chaos. Lasting reward means eradicating the fear that keeps us from a life of awe. This is my core belief as I traverse life and do this E3 work. You will identify your own philosophies all the while honoring clients' viewpoints. Initiating the mystical journey must reflect the philosophies of the client as well as yourself. You will have many opportunities to engage in these discussions the more you do this work and over time, you will find your perception of life changing and evolving.

The process of harmonization as a mystical journey is best explained via three concepts. First, there are specific emotional issues to which all of us have become sensitized and that we work on throughout our entire lives. Second, we make mistakes every day as part of our learning process. This is not inherently a negative thing if growth and learning are the outcomes. Repeating the same mistakes again and again is a powerful stimulus and important feedback mechanism to promote change. Repeated mistakes make the stress warning bells clang loud and clear. Many clients experience something I call the "time ribbon." They identify an emotional issue in its current story line and then discover what the initial sensitizing event and story were. It is very common for clients to come to a great awareness of the countless times where a particular emotional issue came into play. The dots begin to connect for each experience and the fabric of the time ribbon is created. Everything connects from the first sensitizing event to the most recent event. It is very therapeutic for clients to experience this time ribbon.

The third concept in harmonization as a mystical journey is the client's re-creation of themselves through free will. When they choose different behavior in response to a repeated situation, they reinvent their belief systems and perceptions. As the thoughts and consciousness change, so does the physical body. This is what creation through free will is all about. This is the process that changes everything. It is good to discuss with the client these concepts from awakening toward transformation. This type of discussion with my clients is well received.

Chakras and Their Emotions

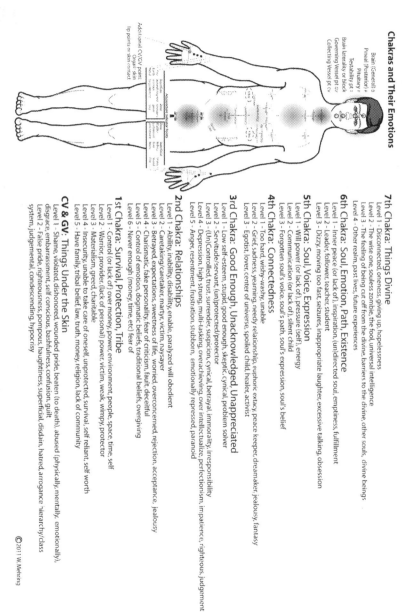

Brain (General)
Pineal (Posterior)
Pituitary
Testability pt
Brain laterality or block
Governing Vessel pt GV
Collecting Vessel pt CV

Additional CV/GV point:
Organ/skin
tip points or skin contact

7th Chakra: Things Divine
Level 1 - Disconnected, oneness, giving up, hopelessness
Level 2 - The wise one, souless zombie, the fool, universal intelligence
Level 3 - The feeling of being cut off from the divine, other souls, divine beings
Level 4 - Other realm, past lives, future experiences

6th Chakra: Soul, Emotion, Path, Existence
Level 1 - Inner peace (or lack of), inspiration, (un)directed soul, emptiness, fulfillment
Level 2 - Leader, follower, teacher, student
Level 3 - Dizzy, moving too fast, seizures, inappropriate laughter, excessive talking, obsession

5th Chakra: Soul, Voice, Expression
Level 1 - Will power (or lack of), pressure (self), energy
Level 2 - Communication (or lack of), silent child
Level 3 - Forgotten soul's voice, soul's path, soul's expression, soul's belief

4th Chakra: Connectedness
Level 1 - Too hard, wishy-washy, unable
Level 2 - Grief, sadness, yearning, needy relationship, euphoric extacy, peace keeper, dreamaker, jealousy, fantasy
Level 3 - Egotist, lover, center of universe, spoiled child, healer, activist
Level 4 - Depression, high strung, multi-tasking, overachieving, over intellectualize, perfectionism, impatience, righteous, judgement
Level 5 - Anger, resentment, frustration, stubborn, emotionally repressed, paranoid

3rd Chakra: Good Enough, Unacknowledged, Unappreciated
Level 1 - Low self-esteem, stupid, good enough, skeptic, cynical, problem solver
Level 2 - Servitude/servant, (un)protected/protector
Level 3 - (Un)Controlled, trust, surrender, suspicion, cynical, betrayal, immorality, irresponsibility
Level 4 - Charismatic, fake personality, fear of criticism, fault, deceitful
Level 5 - Control of emotion, dogmatic beliefs, traditional beliefs, overgiving
Level 6 - Never enough (money, time, etc) fear of

2nd Chakra: Relationships
Level 1 - Ability, inability, disability, enable, paralyzed will obedient
Level 2 - Caretaking/caretaker, martyr, victim, naysayer
Level 3 - Betrayed expectations, sweetness of life, worried, overconcerned, rejection, acceptance, jealousy
Level 4 - Insecurity, unable to take care of oneself, unprotected, survival, self reliant, self worth
Level 5 - Have family, tribal belief, law, truth, money, religion, lack of community

1st Chakra: Survival, Protection, Tribe
Level 1 - Control (or lack of) over money, power, environment, people, space, time, self
Level 2 - Warrior, provider, (lack of personal) power, victim, weak, wimpy, protector
Level 3 - Materialism, greed, charitable
Level 4 - Insecurity, unable to take care of oneself, unprotected, survival, self reliant, self worth
Level 5 - Have family, tribal belief, law, truth, money, religion, lack of community

CV & GV: Things Under the Skin
Level 1 - Shame, violated, dishonored, wounded pride, beaten (to death), abused (physically, mentally, emotionally), disgrace, embarrassment, self conscious, bashfulness, confusion, guilt
Level 2 - False pride, righteousness, pompous, haughtiness, superficial, disdain, hatred, arrogance 'hierarchy/class system, judgemental, condescending, hypocrisy

The Emotional Chakra Chart.

© 2011 W. Mehring

Once the intial dialogue and explanations have occurred, I show the client the E3 Emotional Chakra chart hanging on the wall right next to where I work. Generally, people ask about the colorful balls in different sections of the body which is a great opening for discussion about the chakras and what they stand for. I inform clients that chakras have been described by almost all of the tribal cultures of the world and are thought to be places on our body where we process energy.

This idea of energy processing is different or unusual for many people because not everyone can see these chakra centers. If anything, energy is easier to feel than to see but there are instruments that detect variations in our energy field. These instruments measure the frequency of the wave form in hertz, or cycles per second. The chakras are quite dynamic and the examiner can sense a big difference between a chakra actively processing energy and a chakra where energy flow is 'stuck.'

I explain to the client that I will move my hand along the front of their body, without touching them, to sense areas that are less energy active than others. In areas where energy does not move freely for a long period of time, there is less life force in that area causing the tissues to be more vulnerable to breaking down. There is less vitality in these areas than in others where energy is flowing well. These places of slowed energy indicate areas that need attention during the process of the work.

You will get a positive therapy localization test upon muscle testing when you move your hand over a chakra that is not functioning well. To scan the chakras, move your open palmed hand approximately 18 inches away from the body. If you feel an area with less tingling or less presence, take note. Do a muscle test on something that you know tests strong, a negative test. Then go back to the chakra area where you felt less energy and muscle test again. If the muscle goes weak, you have a positive therapy localization test. If that area does not test positive, then just continue testing until you find the one that is weak. Next, using your kinesthetic sense, feel the difference between the chakra that is normal and the one that is inhibited. There is always something to work on.

The chakras also pick up dysfunction in any of the organs that are part of a chakra's domain. Discuss with the client that organs can process and hold onto stress and highlight common examples such as the following. One person might hold stress in the stomach, which results in ulcers. Another holds stress in the heart, which results in arrhythmias or high blood pressure and so on. It is not necessary to screen every organ, muscle, bone, tissue, and fascia; you just have to screen the seven chakras. That's what makes this process so efficient. Your kinesthetic senses will become honed the more you practice and you will be able to feel these amazing changes. When emotional work is complete in this area, the energy flow returns to normal and the muscle test will no longer be positive.

If the chakras do not test weak, meaning that this is an area that needs attention, then test the extremities. If you still aren't finding any weak or positive tests, make sure the client is able to be tested. If not, have the person drink water and follow the other protocols laid out in Chapter 8. This will include cross crawling, and so on.

B: OPENING

(A) BACKGROUND

Ask religious beliefs, issues of past lives, etc.
-Working within their framework

How muscle tests work. A change of strength.
-Conscious mind/Physical dimension
-Sub/Super conscious mind/Soul dimension

How organs, chakras, or other parts of the body
-Hold and process emotional issues.

Cocreate and discuss the mystical journey
-With the emotional dynamic
-With the players in the story of your life

Initiation of the Mystical Journey
-Specific sensitizing event to your chosen journey
-We must cross a line to learn
-Time ribbon of experiences
-Recreation of self through free choice
-Steps of evolution

(B) OPENING

----Clear yourself, open & connect
----Ask permission to begin working together:
----Testability muscle test: 1) show them their strong; 2)show them their weak

Treatment Possibilities	Places of Pain	Chakra (7-00)	Aura (Templates)	Intuitive Point	Organ	(OTHER)*
Emotional facilitation		○	○	○	○	○
Energetic facilitation		○	○	○	○	○
Vibrational/Sound facilitation		○	○	○	○	○
Vibrational substances Homeopathic, Bach, aroma therapeutic, etc.		○	○	○	○	○
Nutritional fortification Vitamins, foods, supplements, etc.		○	○	○	○	○
Physical Medicine		○	○	○	○	○
Something else Ask Priority of Treatment		○	○	○	○	○
Accupuncture		○	○	○	○	○

*Includes Feelings, Situations, Dreams, Memories...sky's the limit

Detail of E3 Flowchart, A – B.

Opening has two main parts. The first part is to set your intentions and make sure all the circuits are open between you and your client. It is really important to integrate a habit of clearing and creating a sense of neutrality in your thoughts. Silently say, "I want the truth" as your trigger to be neutral, to see yourself as a conduit or catalyst but not the source for the outcomes. Set your intention to connect to the universal consciousness and be open to this help. You can also simply ask for permission to begin working together or to grant permission to start muscle testing.

Have the client drink some water and begin muscle tests. Show the client what their normal arm strength feels like and then touch their testability point (the glabella) on the bridge of their nose, which should cause the muscle to become weaker when tested. This change is muscle test indicates that permission is granted to proceed with testing as all circuits are functioning. If the muscle does not go weak, then refer back to the protocols for establishing testability in Chapter 8. Don't forget to stay light in your heart when working with someone who has never done this before. Your relaxation will assist the client in staying calm and open.

Next, find an access point through a chakra, organ, body area or even through thoughts such as feelings, situations, dreams, and memories that helps you determine what you need to work on, and what treatment is in their highest and best interest. You may not have the tools for many of the treatments, but you'll help the client find out what treatment they need. There are literally limitless places to access the issues within the body. They may be physical, energetic, and are usually emotional. This Opening section of the chart helps you match up areas that need attention with the therapies that will be most beneficial. For example, let's look at a client who presents with chronic headaches. You can put your hand in front of his face, to screen and gain access through the 6th chakra. Perform the muscle test and if the results show therapy localization, you have your access point. Test the concept of a physical component. If the muscle test is a positive, weak muscle test, continue testing ideas and concepts which in this example, led to the headaches caused by a vascular issue. Next, test the concept, "if there is something that can be done," such as dietary changes and nutritional fortification. The test is positive. Test each idea singularly and not combined. Through more testing, it is determined that the person is having an adverse reaction to caffeine; a B complex vitamin would be beneficial. At this point you may think, "AHAHHH, I nailed it." But it may not be over. Continue the testing process to see if anything else is involved. Test the idea "there is something else." This yields a positive muscle test. You must always ask if there is something more because if you don't get uncover all the pieces of the puzzle, the issue will not resolve. In this case, the concept of an emotional component tests positive. The emotional issue that surfaces is not feeling good enough. You and the client bring awareness to the issue and begin the process of harmonization. It is important to remember that there can be several factors leading to a health issue or major stress in the client's life. Always remember to stay open to many possibilities of helping.

Also, keep in mind that you will be working with people who come to you with a physical ailment. The physical ailment can be a result of long-standing, life force energy depletion caused by avoiding dealing with emotional issues. The longer the emotional issues are avoided the more deeply the physical issues can become embedded. Once you deal with the emotional issues and the energy flow returns, it doesn't mean the physical issue will immediately disappear. It will take time enlisting the body's natural healing along with nutrition, homeopathy, exercise, medication and even surgery to resolve the issue. It depends on how far the process has gone. The best time to stop dis-ease is when the energetic roots are shallow, before the dysfunction has manifested in the person's physical body.

This Opening chart is meant to be very flexible. You may start in one of the access points and find several treatment needs and then you find you are led to another treatment area for a different set of treatment needs. Just as many of our emotional issues are linked in a constellation, so can the dis-eases be linked in our bodies. One area of back pain and muscle spasm might be linked to another set of muscles. When one part of the body is coping with a problem, the rest of the body helps to resolve and support body function.

C: DETERMINE THE EMOTIONAL DYNAMIC

Assume that you have either addressed any physical components and worked through treatment possibilities, or there was nothing physical to address. You now focus on the emotional dynamics at play. You ascertain a positive, weak muscle test to the concept of an emotional component. You now need to identify the emotional issue from the list on the chart.

Let's take the example on the chart of the emotional issue of false pride, located in Level 2 of the CV & GV. I choose this example because it is the last thing you would test. Start by testing the concept of chakras 1 through 3. The muscle is strong or negative. Next, test the concept of chakras 4 or 5. Still the muscle is strong/negative. Test the concept of chakras 6 or 7. strong again. Test the concept of CV & GV and the muscle goes weak, signifying a positive test. There are two levels to test in CV&GV, so begin testing the concept of Level 1. The muscle stays strong, so you must continue looking. Test the concept of Level 2 and the muscle goes weak, signifying it is somewhere in Level 2. There are three lines in Level 2, so start with concept line 1 and the muscle goes weak. You now know the issue is in this line. Test the concept of false pride and the muscle goes weak. You have found the right emotional dynamic.

Clients often wonder how their subconscious mind knows what is on each line of that chart. Fractioning the questions down like this means that the universal consciousness within each of us knows everything on the chart. Again, the more you do this work, the more the innate wisdom reveals itself. You are also testing your own intuition. The more your intuition grows, the more you will be asked to use it. For instance, there may come a time when you are told to do an emotional facilitation and find an emotional issue that is not on the chart. When this occurs close your eyes, take a deep breath, and as you exhale wash away any thinking. This shifts you to a moment of complete receiving. Here you will sense the feeling or a sense what the word sounds like. You may see the person in a circumstance and ask in your mind's eye how he or she feels. Sometimes it takes a few moments to download the feeling or image, and experience it yourself. Once you get it, test the concept of that emotion, archetype or situation using a muscle test. Sometimes it is simple and sometimes a little more complex. *Know that you will not be asked to do this unless you are ready.* Most practitioners find everything they need on the chart.

(C) DETERMINE THE EMOTIONAL DYNAMIC

all entry points lead to chakra emotions:

W = Weak
S = Strong
TP = Treatment
Possibilities

Physical or Emotional Entry
becomes weak upon therapy localization

Emotional Facilitation

Test that the emotion
we are working with can be
found in the associated chakra

Test that the emotion
can be found in level ——W—— Test that the emotion
can be found in the ____ chakra

Test for other TP

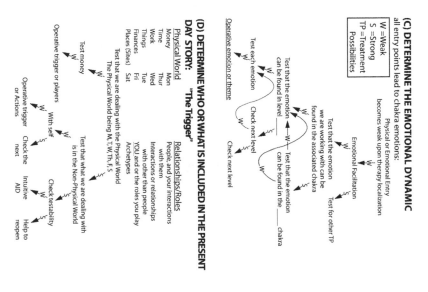

Test each emotion
W
W
Check next level
W
W

Operative emotion or theme

Check next level

(D) DETERMINE WHO OR WHAT IS INCLUDED IN THE PRESENT DAY STORY: "The Trigger"

Physical World
Money — Mon
Time — Tue
Work — Wed
Things — Thur
Finances — Fri
Places (Sites) — Sat

Relationships/Roles
People, and your interactions
with them
Interactions or relationships
with other than people
YOU and or the roles you play
Archetypes

Test that we are dealing with the Physical World
The Physical World being M, T, W, Th, F, S

Test money
W

Operative trigger or players
W

With self
W

Test that what we are dealing with
is in the Non-Physical World

Operative trigger
or Actions

Check the
next

Check testability
W

Intuitive
AID

Help to
reopen

(E) DISTILL AND COMBINE THE EMOTIONAL THEME WITH THE PLAYERS AND DISCOVER THE STORY LINE OF THE CURRENT EVENT

Can you tell me how these two might go together. Keep it
simple. I feel ____ when ____ happened.
W

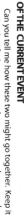

The dynamics of the access story is
AWAKENED

That may be, but it is not the dynamic
for this emotion. Let's try another one.

Rephrase.

Continue self-discovery (remembrance) of how
much this has affected the person.
See how big this really is.

Probe the extent to the point where you see how big this really is for them.
See how this emotional dynamic is involved in so much of their life. You will
use these probing statements when re-testing.

(F) CREATE AN ESSENCE STATEMENT

The emotional dynamic is simply stated and the trigger is
generalized so that it can travel through time and still include
any possibilities of what happened earlier. Muscle test this until
the essence statement is clear and open-ended.

Detail of E3 Flowchart, C – F.

D. DETERMINE WHO OR WHAT IS INCLUDED IN THE PRESENT-DAY STORY

Use the chart categories in this section to find who or what triggers the behavior surrounding an emotion. The first category is Physical World which includes daily world/stuff. The pneumonic for the Physical World are the days of the weeks. The first letter of each of day stands for a category topic. The topics are Monday/Money, Tuesday/Time, Wednesday/Work, Thursday/ Things, Friday/ Finances, places or Saturday/Sites.

The second category is about the non-physical world and is labeled Relationships/Roles.

There are four large categories necessary to cover all the relationships that might come up in your client sessions. The first subcategory includes the clients' relationship and interactions with people. This is generally where most issues are located. If muscle testing yields a positive test, differentiate if the person involved is a relative or a friend. If it is a relative, start testing through father, mother, siblings, husband, wife, children and so on. Most of the time, the trigger is in this subcategory.

The next subcategory includes interactions with pets, and more esoteric relationships such as self/soul other souls and the Divine. Don't be surprised if one of these esoteric triggers comes up. If this occurs, the event usually happened before birth or even before conception. It is important to flush out the story to get a feel for a theme that is underlying in one or perhaps many different situations in your client's current life.

Here is how to navigate this section of the chart. Once you have identified the emotional dynamic from Section C (let's use the issue of control for this example), ask the client, "How do you see this issue or archetype playing out in your life today?" The client is usually well aware of their issue, because they have been working on it for quite some time. The client might say, "I see this issue of control at work with my boss and at home with my wife." The next question is designed to look for the trigger. Ask, "What are the things that trigger you to feel controlled?" Usually your subject gets right to the point on this but if not, continue to use the muscle testing to fill in the missing information.

It is important to test accuracy on this. In this example, as soon as the client says he has control issues at work and at home, test the concept

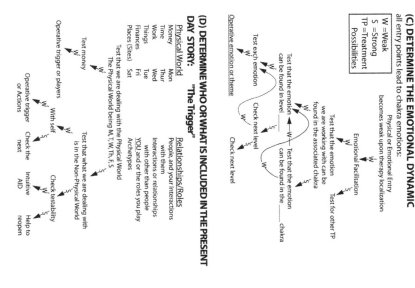

(C) DETERMINE THE EMOTIONAL DYNAMIC
all entry points lead to chakra emotions:

W = Weak
S = Strong
TP = Treatment Possibilities

Physical or Emotional Entry becomes weak upon therapy localization

Emotional Facilitation

Test that the emotion we are working with can be found in the associated chakra

Test that the emotion can be found in level ___

Test that the emotion can be found in the ___ chakra

Test for other TP

Check next level

Check next level

Test each emotion

Operative emotion or theme

(D) DETERMINE WHO OR WHAT IS INCLUDED IN THE PRESENT DAY STORY: "The Trigger"

Physical World
Money — Mon
Time — Thur
Work — Wed
Things — Tue
Finances — Fri
Places (Sites) — Sat

Relationships/Roles
People, and your interactions with them
Interactions or relationships with other than people
YOU and or the roles you play
Archetypes

Test that we are dealing with the Physical World
The Physical World being M, T, W, Th, F, S

Operative trigger or players

Test money

Operative trigger or Actions

Test that what we are dealing with is in the Non-Physical World

With self

Operative trigger or Actions   Check the next

Check testability

Intuitive AID

Help to reopen

(E) DISTILL AND COMBINE THE EMOTIONAL THEME WITH THE PLAYERS AND DISCOVER THE STORY LINE OF THE CURRENT EVENT

Can you tell me how these two might go together. Keep it simple. I feel ___ when ___ happened.

The dynamics of the access story is AWAKENED

That may be, but it is not the dynamic for this emotion. Let's try another one.

Continue self-discovery (remembrance) of how much this has affected the person.

Rephrase.

See how big this really is.

Probe the extent to the point where you see how big this really is for them. See how this emotional dynamic is involved in so much of their life. You will use these probing statements when re-testing.

(F) CREATE AN ESSENCE STATEMENT
The emotional dynamic is simply stated and the trigger is generalized so that it can travel through time and still include any possibilities of what happened earlier. Muscle test this until the essence statement is clear and open-ended.

Detail of E3 Flowchart, C – F.

that what he is talking about is a part of the control issue. In this case, it probably is but there are many times where clients will come up with situations and triggers that bother them, but they do not apply to the issue at hand. Assure the client that while their feelings about these situations are true, they are not germane to the issue you are working on. Make a note of what is said and return to it for further exploration.

E. DISTILL AND COMBINE THE EMOTIONAL THEME WITH THE PLAYERS AND DISCOVER THE STORY LINE OF THE CURRENT EVENTS.

In this section, you distill the theme or motif that is cyclically being repeated in a person's life. As this process unfolds the client begins to see the story line and they become aware of how much these emotional themes are affecting their daily life and their daily decisions. The more aware clients become, the more impatient, if not annoyed, they grow by its presence. They begin to realize how the old belief system is driving their life and bringing with it dysfunction or stress. This is a strong signal to them that this issue needs to be evolved.

F. CREATE AN ESSENCE STATEMENT

Creating an essence statement is the result of the previous section E. The essence statement is a short, concise statement of the emotional dynamic and the trigger. There are many ways of phrasing the essence statement. The simplest way is to use the phrase, "I feel (insert emotional dynamic) when (insert trigger) happens." Sometimes it's wise to bring up the emotional dynamic without the trigger. The best essence statements are clear and open-ended. This example will not work well. "I feel upset and irritated when I see my boss, Fred coming into work like he owns the place." This statement characterizes a complex set of emotions that are superficial if not symptomatic of something much deeper. You will be walking the client back in time to find out when this particular issue began and there is a really good chance that Fred was not there. This phrase is too specific and will not stand through time.

This essence statement will work. "I feel like I am not good enough when I see others as superior." Note the statement didn't say when others act superior and it is centered on the client's reality. It helps the client

(C) DETERMINE THE EMOTIONAL DYNAMIC

all entry points lead to chakra emotions:

| W =Weak |
| S =Strong |
| TP =Treatment |
| Possibilities |

Physical or Emotional Entry
becomes weak upon therapy localization

Emotional Facilitation

Test that the emotion
we are working with can be
found in the associated chakra

Test for other TP

Test that the emotion
can be found in level ——W—— Test that the emotion
can be found in the ____ chakra

Check next level

Test each emotion

Check next level

<u>Operative emotion or theme</u>

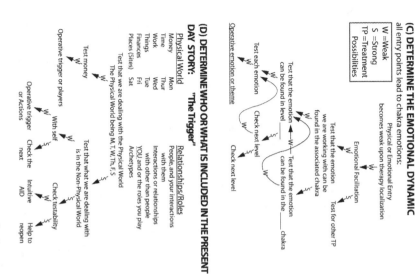

(D) DETERMINE WHO OR WHAT IS INCLUDED IN THE PRESENT DAY STORY: "The Trigger"

<u>Physical World</u>

Money	Mon
Time	Thur
Work	Wed
Things	Tue
Finances	Fri
Places (Sites)	Sat

Test that we are dealing with the Physical World
The Physical World being M, T, W, Th, F, S

<u>Relationships/Roles</u>
People, and your interactions
with them
Interactions or relationships
with other than people
YOU and or the roles you play
Archetypes

Test that what we are dealing with
is in the Non-Physical World

Operative trigger or players

Test money

With self

Check the
next

Operative trigger
or Actions

Intuitive
AID

Check testability

Help to
reopen

(E) DISTILL AND COMBINE THE EMOTIONAL THEME WITH THE PLAYERS AND DISCOVER THE STORY LINE OF THE CURRENT EVENT

Can you tell me how these two might go together. Keep it
simple. I feel _____ when _____ happened.

The dynamics of the access story is
AWAKENED

That may be, but it is not the dynamic
for this emotion. Let's try another one.

Continue self-discovery (remembrance) of how
much this has affected the person.
See how big this really is.

Rephase.

Probe the extent to the point where you see how big this really is for them.
See how this emotional dynamic is involved in so much of their life. You will
use these probing statements when re-testing.

(F) CREATE AN ESSENCE STATEMENT

The emotional dynamic is simply stated and the trigger is
generalized so that it can travel through time and still include
any possibilities of what happened earlier. Muscle test this until
the essence statement is clear and open-ended.

Detail of E3 Flowchart, C – F.

see their part in how they perceive the world. It also means that they are in control of changing their own interpretation of others' actions. The essence statement could also be "I feel insecure around others." This is even more simplified without including the trigger. The best essence statement for that client will be indicated by the weakest/positive muscle test. If they were to choose a statement like, "I feel inferior when others strut their stuff," the muscle would probably still go weak and be a positive test, but it might be a "betweener." The muscle will be weak, yet not really weak. Keep distilling the essence statement down until the arm is demonstrably weak. Once you have this you can go onto the next step.

G. DETERMINE THE TIMELINE OF THE ORIGINAL SENSITIZING EVENT

Begin by testing the idea that there is an original sensitizing event. Include the phrase, "an event where you felt (insert emotion) when (insert trigger) happened." You can also ask about the original sensitizing test without include the trigger. This leaves your search more generalized. If the sensitizing event is indeed recent, then just harmonize it and the current events and assess whether or not you need to check for future probabilities. If the muscle goes weak/a positive test in response to the question of an original sensitizing event, then continue on to find the timeline where this issue first began, going back in blocks of five years at a time.

Let's say that the sensitizing event occurred at age six. Start with testing the idea that the initial sensitizing event was from conception to age five. If the muscle stays strong/a negative test, test the idea that the initial sensitizing event was between age six and ten or you can say, "Up to the age of ten." If the muscle test is weak/positive, test the idea of age six again and if the muscle is weak/positive, you found the age where the event occurred. People often remember events in reference to school so it is usually helpful to find out what grade the client was in at a particular age. Remember, clients will be in two different grades for each year of their life.

To best understand the issue, one must imagine what the world looked and felt like at that age. You can't apply how you feel about

(G) DETERMINE THE TIME LINE OF THE ORIGINAL SENSITIZING EVENT

"Let's test the idea of the earliest sensitizing event where you felt _____ when _____."

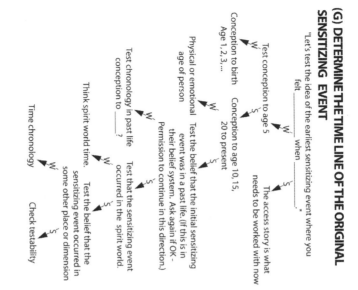

Test conception to age 5   Conception to age 10, 15, 20 to present

The access story is what needs to be worked with now

Conception to birth
Age 1, 2, 3, ...

Physical or emotional age of person   Test the belief that the initial sensitizing event was in a past life. (If this is in their belief system. Ask again if OK - Permission to continue in this direction.)

Test chronology in past life conception to ____?

Test that the sensitizing event occurred in the spirit world.

Think spirit world time.   Test the belief that the sensitizing event occurred in some other place or dimension

Time chronology   Check testability

(H) EXPERIENCE AND EXPAND THE ORIGINAL SENSITIZING EVENT

Expand and explore how the **Emotional Dynamic** played itself out with the **Trigger** in the original sensitizing event. (You will need to repeat **D** to determine the original sensitizing trigger.) Use probing statements to 1) determine the extent of the emotional dynamic in the original sensitizing event. 2) determine how the plot of the present day issue connects or parallels with the original sensitizing event.

Detail of E3 Flowchart, G – H.

something as an adult to how you felt about it as a three year old. Keep in mind that our biggest issues usually occur from conception to age six. Issues can actually originate in utero. If the timeline muscle testing from conception to birth yields a positive test, you can isolate between first, second and third trimesters. This is important as there are distinct developmental differences for each of these trimesters. During the first trimester, we grow from a single cell to developing a spinal cord, neurological tissue, the beginning of eyes, and buds for feet and hands. In some ways, we look more like an amphibian than a biped. What is the consciousness of that child and what are the issues that may arise during this stage of development? There may be several different perspectives that you can't anticipate. The conscious mind and the soul of this fetal human are both present so there are two different perspectives and issues that will come into play.

If clients are looking through the experience of the soul animating the body, the issues can commonly be about feeling disconnected. As the soul is merging into the physical body, it has to lose some of its connection with the Creator. This is particularly true of Green personalities. They feel a longing when they leave the experience of being one with Creation. Clients will talk about experiencing being a part of an interconnection with all souls and all consciousness before they are grounded in the physical realm. When their consciousness becomes more grounded, they experience feelings of loss, grief and disconnection. These clients can feel quite hopeless in situations that awaken these old feelings.

Clients also may have co-experienced what the mother was experiencing as fetus and mother are very connected at that point. The issues may come to them in the energetic download or even through the proximal energetic field of the family, especially the mother. There may also have been more than one egg released during ovulation. Multiple eggs can be fertilized at the same time, not to mention the phenomenon of twins. It is not uncommon for a less vital embryo to die and be reabsorbed so emotional issues of loss, grief, or abandonment for the surviving embryo can be rooted in this first trimester time.

Many of the bodily systems become fully developed in the second trimester. The older and more developed the fetus becomes, the more there is a shift to human consciousness issues rather than the soul's perspective.

During early development, the consciousness is not very connected to the baby's brain because it is so undeveloped.

The third trimester is really about the fetus developing into a being that can exist outside the womb. There are some issues of the soul in this time period as well as the co-experiences with the parents but in general, the issues rooted in the third trimester start to reveal what that person will work on the rest of their physical human existence.

To determine the timeframe for the original sensitizing event you may test people from conception all the way to their current age and still not obtain a positive muscle test. When this happens, test the idea of the issue originating in a past life. If this a positive muscle test occurs, follow the guidelines and timeline of the initial sensitizing event in that past life. If the age of the original sensitizing event is older than age six, there is a chance that you are getting a picture of how the issue manifested in the later part of that life. Once you know more about how the issue affects them in the older part of that life, re-check and see if it timelines to an even younger age. This can be done by testing the idea of an earlier sensitizing event when the person felt (insert emotion) when (insert trigger) happened.

Essentially, you start with a current event in the past life just as you would with someone in a present life, and regress back to the initial event, in that past life. Treat the past life just like you were testing the present life. Start with how the issue affected them when they are older and then move back to the earlier time when the issue began. Past life connections are not uncommon. It's reasonable to think that we do not always complete harmonizing all the emotional issues in this lifetime. This work may not require going back to an initial sensitizing event in a previous life, but sometimes it does. Whatever is needed will present itself.

H. EXPERIENCE AND EXPAND THE ORIGINAL SENSITIZING EVENT

This is where you explore the situation where the client grabbed on to this emotional dynamic with all of its triggers. You will look for the connection between that event and the current events that carry this theme. You have determined the age when the issues started and have developed an essence statement that describes the situation. Simply ask the client "Was there anything that happened at age _____that you can remember where you felt _____when _____happened?"

If the person cannot remember an event, ask if someone in the family remembers any family history or events. You will be surprised how buried memories bubble to the conscious mind during this process. The first few years of life are very hard to remember so the older the client was at the time of the sensitizing event, the more likely they are to remember it. If the memory just seems to pop up out of nowhere, there is a very good chance that it is the sensitizing event. It just works that way. However, there are people that just don't remember a lot of their childhood. If a client had a very rough life, it is common to simply shut it out. But you have a secret weapon that will allow you to access this. Just repeat step D to find the trigger and anything else that helps round out the story. Think of it as playing a game of twenty questions to learn what happened.

I: EXPERIENCING AND EVOLVING THE EXPERIENCE

As you explore the original sensitizing event you have already begun Step I: Experiencing and Evolving the Experience. There is something very important about how we perceive reality. We give the same credibility and power to experiences even when we encounter those experiences in different states of consciousness; the waking state, dream state, imagination, or a hypnotic state. This means we can employ these different states, particularly the hypnotic state, to investigate and rewrite life experiences. Hypnosis becomes an invaluable tool in guiding clients through the steps of evolution.

The hypnotic state is maintained when the client is relaxed and the tester and surroundings are calm. You will ask the client to sit back in a comfortable chair and place their hands on the area where you found the issue. If the issue was not bodily pain in a specific area, but was a feeling, or a memory or some other ailment, use your kinesthetic feel or muscle tests to find where exactly it is being stored in the body. If you wish to bypass this, just have the client put one hand on the heart and the other on the forehead. This default position works because the mind and the heart are our two largest emotional processing centers and one of these will connect to where the issues are stored.

(I) EVOLVING AND EXPERIENCING EVENT

STEP 1
AWAKENING
SELF-REMEMBRANCE — Allow the client to experience this initial sensitizing event.
Acknowledging/Breathing/Releasing

STEP 2
SELF-REMEMBERANCE — Allow them to really reveal the dynamic of this event.

STEP 3
AWARENESS — Allow them to open up to the time ribbon that connects the many experiences in their life where this emotional dynamic has been operating. Ex: See how it has played itself out from each chakra's point of view and then experience the many layers of the belief system.

"Once the wish for change is united with being able to see the past behaviors, the seeds of a new dynamic are created.

TRANSITION — See yourself in this situation using the principles of evolution, the strengths and experiences of this life and other infinite lives as you revisit the same situation. Allow this to unfold and evolve over and over again until new dialogue and new outcomes are created.

STEP 4
TRANSFORMATION — Ask the person to reveal how the experience unfolded. As they do, listen for incongruity with principles of evolution and/or muscle test.

STEP 5 — The person can at any time return back to evolve the outcome and do additional work.

Eyes open to future probabilities - Utilizing intuitive aid and insight ask the person, "If this dynamic were to recreate itself in your future, how might it come up?"

STEP 6 — (Permission) Test if it's OK to view future possibilities for the purpose of evolving. Test if it's beneficial.

Muscle test/intuit that that experience is beneficial in evolving this emotional dynamic.

STEP 7 — Through the mind's eye, evolve through the future probability utilizing all new dynamics and tools. Make as many transformative sweeps as needed.

Ask the person to reveal how the experience unfolded. As they do, listen for incongruity with principles of evolution and/or muscle test.

STEP 8
(INFORMATION) — This is the place of final preparation before this dynamic manifests itself in the physical world.

Freewill in the physical world. The person must take a step where they have never gone in the physical world. Know that this step will be difficult. It will be saddled with some of their greatest fears.

STEP 9
(INFORMATION)
TRANSMUTATION — "The lessons will continue to manifest until the dynamic has completely changed and there is no hesitation to take the new step.

A new feeling of Strength and Grace that replaces fear.

A new emotional dynamic is in place and the old situation stops manifesting.

STEP 10 — Test the original emotion, original, current & future triggers and previously active probing statements.

Test concept of accompanying emotion.   Test the idea of the next emotion.

Return to (C)   Test original emotion   Return to (C)   Check testability
W   W   W   W

Return to TPs   Return to TPs   Re-open Go back to original emotion
W   W

Find part missed   Go to TPs or testability   Test for completion

Detail of E3 Flowchart, I.

170

Another option is to just allow clients to relax in the chair with their arms to the side. If you are unsure which technique to use, you can confirm through muscle testing the best approach. If you have training as a hypnotherapist, doing an induction into a deep hypnotic state will be of great benefit. If you do not have this training, you can easily induce a mild state of hypnosis for your clients in the following manner. Have the clients close their eyes and relax. Speak slowly, pause between sentences and allow your voice to become more monotone and soft as if you were lulling a small child to sleep. Ask the client to relax and clear their mind. Invite them to take a moment to just feel their breath moving in and out. Ask them to take inventory of their body and to release and loosen up any places where they feel tightness or tension. If the issue at hand was found in a specific body area, you can ask them to concentrate on the feel of this area and allow it to become very loose and free. Finally, give them the suggestion that as they breathe, they will be breaking up the old beliefs and reactions. As they breathe in, they bring in new behaviors, and as they exhale, they let go of the past. Use these words as a starting place. You will develop a language that works for you as you help clients in this process of with experiencing and evolving.

Continue the technique by asking the client to begin seeing the initial sensitizing event where they experienced _____ while _____ happened. Tell the client to imagine the experience and allow it to become full. Anything that the imagination brings up with will be valuable to the process. Even if they can't remember it, often times their imagination re-creates it perfectly because the memories are still stored somewhere intact. When this occurs, they have started the process of awakening. Ask them to feel their emotions deeply while they are experiencing this event. Have them go slowly and continue to encourage them to allow the experience to fill out. New things may come into the picture that they didn't see the first time the event opened. Remind them again to be open to what they are experiencing at that time in their life and how it feels in the area where the emotions are being processed. While this is happening, the person is deeply in self-remembrance. They not only remember who they are and who they really want to be, but they are analyzing the experience and are beginning to see who they can become.

Ask the client to become aware of all the incidents from the initial event to the present and how the belief or event shaped their actions and experiences. Sometimes this begins automatically without the suggestion which illustrates how important this step is. Encourage them to look deeper at whatever situation comes to mind and see if this belief system somehow altered what happened that day. This stage is awareness, where clients see how their emotional issue is connected to their life decisions and perceptions. They may feel like this issue is in everything. This is when they create the time ribbon where they see the connections and laminations that have occurred around this belief system. The more aware clients are of how invasive this unproductive belief is, the quicker they want to change it. When they make the choice to change, the stage of transition is over. They have climbed up to the peak and are now walking down the other side of the mountain. Use this metaphor because the difficult work is now done. It has taken a large part of their life to get to this point. Choosing to change takes a lot of stress and dissatisfaction. The momentum of inertia can be a formidable force to redirect, but the point is that they are doing it *now.*

The next stage of transformation lasts beyond the session because the client will continue to evolve their belief systems. You will ask your clients to see once again the initial sensitizing event, only this time remind the client that they have the freedom to change it. Ask them to bring all their wisdom and life experience. Remind them to see who they really are and who they want to be, before finding a new way to walk into this important experience. The moment they change this experience, everything that follows in their present life also changes. It is imperative to make sure that the new path doesn't have any land mines or negative karma. Set up a new belief system that doesn't create other problems using the guidelines in Chapter 6, The Basic Four and More, and the Twenty-five Principles in Chapter 7. This particular step is the key to the E3 process. Creating a new path that can take away the stress in life and replace it with a harmonious path.

Ask the clients to softly narrate how they traversed the experience. Listen to what they say and if there is something you feel will not work. Help them add more clarity to the newly evolved path. Help them reshape this experience . If at first you are unsure, simply muscle test after each small segment of the re-creation story. If the muscle stays strong/a negative test, feverything is still good. Only test one new response to the experience at a time. If there is more than one action when you muscle test, the result will not be clear. Have them go through the entire story with your senses on high or muscle testing along the way. If the muscle goes weak, call on the innate, your inner wisdom as well as the client's, to continually evolve the experience until it is clear of any future negative repercussions. Again, this is a process that continues beyond your session. The client will remember this work when the issue or the trigger comes up again. It is part of the transformation process for a client to imagine how their issues come up in their daily experience, and then choose to change it. Transformation is truly indicative of a person being on the path of evolution.

It is not uncommon for clients to feel unsure or uncomfortable with their new behaviors and actions. It is important for them to develop tools for healthy dialogue when working through an issue or discussing their feelings. When working through the E3 protocols, the client will revisit an initial sensitizing event. They will understand the emotional dynamic behind the present-day situation. The people and triggers present in the original experience will be discovered. The patient will re-experience the event deeply and feelings will inevitably surface. This allows them to be aware of all motivations, strategies and underlying beliefs, both their own and those of the other people involved in the dynamic. Then the client will re-create the experience so they can change their actions. This cements their new belief system. Whenever possible, there is a discussion with the person who participated in the initial event. As a facilitator, you will assist the client in this dialogue. Here are some helpful guidelines.

The client expresses their commitment to the dialogue and the relationship. This can be as simple as them stating, "I am committed to our relationship and I wish for us to talk and work this out. Do you?" This lets the client know if they have a willing partner in the process. If the answer is yes, then all parties are committed to the process and the relationship.

Instruct your patients to always be constructive in their dialogue. It is completely acceptable and often preferred that people express themselves passionately and if need be, loudly. However, harmful words followed by apologies, only work once. If this pattern becomes cyclic in nature, it can become abusive. Also encourage your client to avoid name-calling or telling anyone else how to act or feel. Notice when a client says the word "you." This waves a red flag because they are probably blaming someone. A blame statement is, "You make me feel bad when you call me names." There is no assigning blame, guilt or shame. The more productive statement would be "I feel insecure when anyone calls me names." It is important to instill in the client that taking responsibility for their actions will create a neutrality that allows for empathy and compassion of unguarded, pure emotions. It is only here that people will find the understanding and desire to make a long-term change in their behavior. Using guilt or shame will change some people's actions, but for only a short period of time. Heart-to-heart dialog is where healthy transformations reach the core beliefs of a person's matrix.

We all create our responses and therefore have the power to alter them. This is about choice. A person is free to craft a totally different outcome and response the next time they encounter the same situation. This puts the responsibility on the client as well as giving them the power to manifest life changes. You may hear a client say they had no choice in responding in the way that they did. It is your job as the facilitator to show them this is simply not true but that there is some belief deep within them that makes their conditioned response seem like the best alternative. This is an important point in the therapy. If the facilitator can really get them to see that every action they take is their choice, they can choose new patterns as easily as they can follow the old behaviors.

Another important parameter is to instruct your clients not to fall into the trap of justifying their behavior. Logic to justify feelings or position creates something to be argued about. Often times, the other person in the dynamic wins a battle of wits which only takes the client further away from their feelings and message. Encourage your client to discuss feelings, not to use logic to argue or defend a position.

It is also important for the client to speak succinctly using as few words as necessary to convey their message. Compounding all of the emotions makes it more difficult to focus on what is important. For example, clients can say, "I feel sadness when the people I am in a relationship with are withdrawn." Or "I feel unimportant when I feel someone is lying to me." Or "I feel unlovable when I think people are lying to me." The more words clients use the less impact they will have. Instruct the client to make their statement as brief as possible; no more than ten words. The longer the sentence, the less impact their expression of feelings will have.

Employing these guideline as you harmonize the initial sensitizing event will increase your success. Generally, you ask the patient to connect to the other person's consciousness and speak their words. This is like role playing between the client as themselves and the client as the other person. Putting yourself in the other person's shoes provides insight into the other person's motivations. This also creates very humanistic moments of understanding and acceptance. If you are trained or have become skilled in hypnotherapy, I recommend this deeper work on the more entrenched issues. However, transformation will still work if you choose to use guided imagery coupled with the patient's imagination. You can lead the client through a guided imagery of the dialogue inviting the client to narrate what happens step by step. This can be distracting for some people since they are viewing the incident in their mind's eye. There are those, however, who like to tell the story while it's happening. The second method is to instruct the client in the process, let them play out the dialogue in their head and then recount to you about the process when it's over. Make sure to hear the whole dialogue to make sure the client is not creating new problems. As always, use all the guidelines, principles and your inner wisdom to oversee the interaction. Remember that you can always use muscle testing to ensure that the reformation process you have chosen is a good one. If the muscle stays strong, then everything is okay. If the muscle goes weak, then there is something that isn't quite right. Continue to evolve the experience until you find all the right words and actions for re-creating the event.

Clients will learn to use the same guidelines in every day interactions. The more they practice events in their thoughts, the better they will be when the event happens in the physical world. They may also get a chance to practice it in future probabilities. Integrating their new beliefs and actions into events as they happen completes the transformation process. If they don't do it quite right, that's okay because they can always reframe. They may realize the error shortly after the event or even the next day.

Welcome to being human. The important part is that they caught the mistake. They can simply go back to the person and say, "Yesterday when I was talking to you about my feelings" or "yesterday when I was _____, I was not okay with what I did. If I could do it again differently, this is what I would do. My motivations for doing it the other way were _____. Thanks for listening." They can customize the language, of course, but picture it as the essence of the conversation. The important thing is that clients are earnestly searching for the motivations behind every one of their actions. They also must become aware of when their old conditioned words or actions surface. The habit or addiction must simply be broken. Stress and chaos can be triggers for old actions or speech to resurface. Signs can include elevated heart rate and blood pressure, stomachaches, headaches, a feeling in the belly or a taste in the mouth. These are the clues to guide patients away from the old patterns. The body is tired of continually repairing the effects of stress. The body and the soul want to support this work.

J. TEST THE NEED FOR FUTURE PROBABILITIES

What happens in our future is quite dependent upon all the decisions we have made in our past. It sometimes makes the future look almost like fate. Part of the E3 process is using future probabilities as a tool for learning and growth. Imagine what an advantage it would be in sports to know all the plays that the opposition is going to use before the game even starts. This is what future probabilities are all about but it is not only this. Knowing future probabilities can indicate that the more the person changes their behaviors and actions in the present, the less likely the event that they are working with needs to happen.

If you get a weak/positive test in response to testing for future probabilities repeat Step D, finding out who and what is involved, as a future probability. Look for who or what will trigger the event. Keep using the muscle tests, the person's input, and your own intuition to fill out what will happen in the future. Once you find it, have the patient work out the new actions that are the end result of their new belief. For example, a client is working on an abandonment issue and you ascertain a positive test to look into future probabilities. You would then test to see who are the people involved. Imagine it is the client's mother. Then test to see when the event will occur and it shows up to be on Christmas morning. Through further testing, you find out that the mother doesn't like the gift you purchased for her and she leaves the room. The trick here is not buy a different gift in anticipation of this event but to correlate how the story of the original sensitizing event triggers the old belief systems and actions that result in the feeling of abandonment. An important step in evolving this situation is to determine what actions you might take to work this out. Being OK with the mother pulling away is the first step and the second step is to really embrace the persistent connection that children feel with their parents even if this is on a soul level. An the final step is to be poised to ask the mother for a dialog about feeling and expectations. The act of working things out will bring the client and her mother closer. This can reverse the abandonment into a deeper sense of connection.

Whenever the client is recreating situations in their mind's eye, this is done in a mild hypnotic state. The longer they stay with this, the deeper they will venture into this brainwave state that allows access to their inner wisdom as well as allowing their abilities to change. This is easier than you think and I will address techniques for this in subsequent chapters. you have harmonized this event, test to see if there is another.

It is interesting when clients return and share how everything played out just as the muscle testing predicted. The closer to the event when you are using future probabilities, the more likely the event may occur. The other thing that can happen is that everybody shows up to the event just as it was foreseen but the trigger does not occur. The story line will have changed slightly. In that moment, it is possible the work done in that hypnotic state was so deep, that the client no longer attracted that situation. It may also be that the client's beliefs transformed so much between the session and the future probability that they no longer needed that lesson. The future is a probability that is always changing. Whatever the underpinnings of time might be, the use of future probabilities is a great tool. It is a great learning tool to exercise how to become free of old unwanted belief systems.

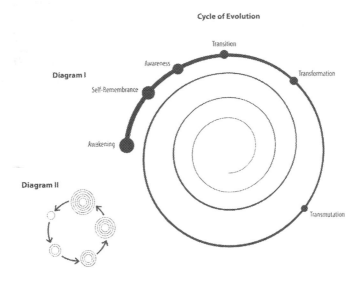

SPIRAL CHART OF EVOLUTION

The process of evolution is depicted by a large spiral. As we travel the cycles of evolution, the intensity and the difficulty of the process decrease. Although the issues become fainter, they never completely go away. We act and behave differently in response to a trigger, proving to the universe that we have resolved this issue. We have evolved despite having the faint memory of old behaviors. These moments are rewarding as we connect to where we came from and our own capacity to change our lives for the better. We may remember the first time we walked directly into our fear with open arms, ready to see and accept ourselves for who we are. Acceptance is always part of the journey because when we accept ourselves, others and every experience of life, we have arrived. When something happens that would have once triggered us into chaotic feelings or compelled us to tell others how poorly we were treated and how bad life can be, we instead accept the experience and do the best we can.

To complete an E3 session, it is important to muscle test that a particular emotional dynamic is harmonized. You can simply say, "Test the idea of (insert the emotional dynamic)." If the muscle is strong, you are done with that emotion. You can also retest each of the triggers or any of the old stories. If the muscle stays strong when you talk about these stories, this indicates the work is complete for the day. I say "for the day" because you will likely revisit a particular issue many times in order to make clients continually aware of their issues and their new responses and behaviors. If they do not do this work, the emotional dynamic will resurface once again. It may resurface in a slightly different form, but it will resurface. It is helpful to instruct the client to keep a small notebook with them at all times and jot down when the emotional issue comes up and what their new response was. Tell them you want to hear about their experiences and continue to give them some tools to stay aware of the work they are doing. This notepad practice is meant to be a reminder for awareness throughout the day like tying a string around their finger.

You will also test the idea of linked emotions before ending the E3 session. If the muscle test is weak/positive to the question of a linked emotion, return to Step C: Determining the Emotional Dynamic, and begin the process again. If the muscle stays strong, then touch or therapy localize to the place where this was stored or where you started in the very beginning. Touch that area. If the muscle is strong, you have covered all your bases testing each of the issues, triggers and access points that you used to access the issues to begin with. In a sense, you are just backing out and making sure that everything has been dealt with completely. Think of it like closing all the open windows on your computer screen as you are saving information and shutting down for the day. This completes the E3 process.

CHAPTER 11

WHAT IT TAKES TO BE AN EFFECTIVE E3 PRACTITIONER

PRACTITIONERS WHO ARE NOT TRAINED as psychologists may be intimidated by the psychological nature of this work; however, the E3 process is not difficult. The best practitioners are honed by the school of life rather than formal education. To be the most effective E3 practitioner you must:

- Become familiar and confident with muscle testing.
- Learn the flow of the charts and seamlessly transition from one step to the next.
- Embrace the flexibility within the E3 process as you gain experience.
- Use all of the E3 guidelines, principles and philosophies to support and keep your client focused and on track.
- Ask questions that facilitate the client's self-awareness, feelings, motivations, and honesty.
- Speak less and listen more. Be present by setting a clear intention that you are harmonizing the client's needs, not your own.
- Keep the essence statement broad and generalized so that it applies to all situations.

Effective practitioners are also involved in the exciting adventure of *returning* through self-discovery. Returning is honoring one's true nature and returning to the land of the soul. This happens when we stop wanting to be like anyone else and accept our radically unique self. We listen to the soul's wisdom and walk through life in awe and finding peace in chaos. The most effective E3 practitioners have engaged and struggled with their own issues. By working tirelessly on their own "stuff," E3 practitioners can effectively guide others. This applies to practitioners that have formal therapeutic training as well. Therapists do their best work when they are in touch with their own subconscious thoughts and the motivations behind their own actions. Isolating and calming the ego mind's chatter is essential when guiding clients in the work, as is letting go of your own issues while listening and guiding the client. The first session will not be perfect as the E3 process takes practice to develop skill and confidence. But actually, perfection has no place in client sessions. This is why it's called practicing. The key is to be present for the client and for the inner wisdom or innate to come through.

The biblical account of Moses receiving the Ten Utterances (oft translated as Ten Commandments) at Mount Sinai gives us some insight into the innate, inner wisdom. Moses says to the Source, "When I come to the Israelites and say to them "the God of your ancestors has sent me to you," and they ask me "What is God's name?" what shall I say to them?" The answer is "Eh'yeh Asher Eh'ye - I am becoming that which I am becoming." The Divine name is a verb not a noun. As a part of our creative, self-healing endeavors, we too are becoming that which we will become. Our journey is one of endless becoming. We encounter the innate in our relationships and encounters all the time. I was once showing a house to a prospective renter. We were chatting during the interview process and I asked what kind of work he did. The man told me he was a career soldier but looked away when he said he'd been to Iraq. It was clear he was holding something in and he began to cry when I asked if he was okay. He told me he had been a helicopter pilot in Desert Storm, during the first invasion. He shared his entire story of how he gunned down civilians as well as Iraqi soldiers, as they walked back from Kuwait to Iraq. He was ordered to fire even though the civilians were women and young men. He was later honored as a military hero for his actions. As I sat with him, he sobbed, saying, "I don't know why I am telling you all this. You just seem like someone I can talk to." All I did was ask about his work and if he was OK, without judgment or comment. Because I was a neutral listener and present to the innate, he felt safe to share his inner pain. The innate works that simply. That soldier called me later to say he was deciding whether he was going to stay in the military or not so he would not be renting the house. He told me how much better he felt after our talk and then I never heard from him again. I was happy to have participated in his defining moment when the difference between his behavior and the true inner wisdom of the soul became clear. This discovery made it difficult for him to follow orders from societal authorities that violated his inner wisdom.

In review, effective E3 practitioners are present, not judgmental. They ask questions that bring awakening and awareness to the client's chaotic issues and stress. They listen more than they talk. Most importantly, they do their own harmonization work, teach from experience, quiet the ego, and draw from life's events as well as the soul's knowledge. By following these steps, practitioners will attract the clients that they can best help, regardless where the practitioner is in their own life.

PART III

Chapter 12

REFLECTIVE SELF-ESTEEM VERSUS INTERNAL SELF-ESTEEM

Reflective self-esteem is solely based on what other people think of us, whether that perception is positive or negative. Internal self-esteem reflects a feeling of wholeness and self-acceptance that is immune to outside opinions. What we think of ourselves is comprised of a ratio of both of these aspects of self-esteem. We become more accepting of ourselves as we learn from life's experiences, and as we do this, we walk towards a peaceful life.

Our family of origin is the most important contributor to our internal self-esteem. Internal self-esteem is what parents most want to instill in their children, yet this is impossible unless the parent possesses that sense of wholeness and self-acceptance themselves. My mother wisely told me that her greatest gift to me was her many years of psychotherapy. My mother became consumed with fear, anger and doubt after the two people she cared for the most in her life, her husband and her father, died just a few months apart. She also had to take care of a child who was under the age of one. If she did not have a piece of this internal wholeness already embedded within her, she would never have had the power to continue on with her life. It gave her the mighty strength to become a warrior of change as well as instilling in me that same sense of internal self-esteem which put me squarely on the healing path. I am reminded again of the story of the Hasidic master, the Ba'al Shem Tov. His father also instilled knowledge of wholeness, enabling the Ba'al Shem Tov to walk into his darkest fears with his arms open, able to transform fear into awe.

Those who benefit from the emotional work done by previous generations begin their life journey with introspective self-esteem. If they continue on this path, they experience life in awe. Those who live in fear will contend with the constant chasing of reflective self-esteem. Nonetheless, life provides us with many opportunities to transform this fear-based reflective self-esteem to a reverence-based internal self-esteem.

Being aware of our personal reflective self-esteem means asking the following questions. "What do I do to gain the approval or acceptance of others?" "How do I act to elicit a favorable response from the person I am trying to impress?" When we feel whole, there is no reason to manipulate others into telling us how good we are. Reflective self-esteem is constantly covering up our sense that we aren't good enough. A life driven by the ego is a life full of comparisons and hierarchies. The ego never tires of hoisting us up and pushing others down in countless categories of assessment and judgment. In addition, this external reflective view lives and dies by the ego's scorecard, constantly grasping for safety and feeling good enough. Our speech is even filled with attempts to persuade others of how good we are. If we're not persuading others, then we are convincing ourselves. A blanket of silence would fall across the land if the ego stopped its sales routine for just one day.

The more you have reflective self esteem, the more you try to push your fears into the darkest corners of consciousness. These are the actions and beliefs that society deems unacceptable. An example of this would be a young boy who upon entering puberty, explores his normal sexual curiosity by looking at Playboy magazine. If he is punished or harshly scolded or humiliated in front of others about this behavior, his normal sexual development may be negatively impacted. He will think he is a bad person for having normal sexual thoughts. This is a classic example of someone with a shadow formation. A shadow can incorporate feelings of not being good enough manifested in abandonment, betrayal and many other issues.

Where reflective self-esteem is ego-based, internal self-esteem is soul-based. Our soul knows that it is complete and that it is a part of something so infinite and far sighted that there is no need for worry and fear. The following chapter will give you a clear picture of internal self-esteem.

Chapter 13

THE EGO'S SCORECARD: EGO VERSUS SOUL PERSPECTIVE

THE EGO'S SCORECARD IS SO insidious that we forget how much it drives us. We spend most of our life chasing to get a win, striving to get an A+ grade. Yet, it is all an illusion because those scores and grades are based on others' opinions. We learn from our parents, our culture and our society what behaviors and actions score high and what score low. For example, plus-size women in Samoa earn an A+ as that body type is considered the epitome of beauty. In Western culture, however, the opposite is true with fashion models and television personalities being rail thin. The adage, "you can never be too thin and or too rich" is the mantra.

The verbal and nonverbal schooling begins early on. As children, we are thirsty to be loved, cared for, and safe and we immediately learn which behaviors merit reward and which punishments. So we mold and change ourselves to receive the rewards and to avoid negative consequences. These early lessons are the blackboard where the ego posts the scores. We become trained to focus on the hierarchical ladder in every situation, our placement on the rungs telling us where we are in relation to others. The ego is bolstered the higher we are up the ladder and we get that A+. The ego equates A+ with nirvana.

This A+ grade is a combination of our interpretation of events and our body's neurochemical response. Negative neurochemicals wave red flags whereas the release of positive neurochemicals keep you on track. The more positive neurochemicals are released, the more we want this chemical response to occur. This is why we repeat certain behaviors. When we excel at something, we concentrate our efforts there. If this sounds like addiction and addictive behavior, that's because it is.

Reflective self-esteem and the ego's scorecard go hand-in-hand. Here is an example about an amazing young athlete, Josh, and his father, Steve. Steve did not have an easy childhood. He was not gifted in school; his family was not rich nor was he the best-looking guy on campus. What he did have was athleticism. This is where he could compete.

So compete he did. Steve's parents supported his playing football and, though he was a natural athlete, in the beginning he did not play well. Every time he made a little mistake, the coach pulled him out of the game. He could not stand this. Imagine the negative neurochemical release. The coach told Steve that if he wanted to improve his game, he needed to practice two hours every day. And to make matters worse, on days when he was unsuccessful on the football field, Steve's father would drop him off a mile from home and make him walk the rest of the way: negative neurochemical release. If there were another avenue to positive reinforcement, he definitely would have taken it.

All of the men in Steve's family fit the Red personality. Steve practiced two hours a day because he was a warrior and loyal to the family. He began to receive praise from his father as his playing improved: positive neurochemical release. But there were still those days when Steve didn't come out on top of the game that he had to walk the last mile home. The message was simple: domination equals positive reinforcement and positive chemical release and weakness equals negative. This is how the sins of the parents become the sins of the children.

When he became a parent, Steve and his wife Nancy actively supported sports for their four sons. Jim, their oldest boy, was the star of the high school football team. The second oldest, Philip, attempted to play football, and then hockey, but the arts were his true calling. The two youngest children, Andrew and Josh were witness to their father's response to Jim and Phillip' choices. Jim's football prowess garnered positive praise, but Philip's artistic skill did not. They saw how their father ignored Philip. Phillip was very close to his mother who accepted her son's choice.

Steve's self-esteem was intimately connected to his children's athletic abilities. When they dominated other players, the same positive neurochemical release would occur for Steve as it did when he played football as a young athlete. So for Steve, anything less than the best performance, even second place, was not acceptable. Jim, his oldest son, applied for scholarships to all of the top colleges, was turned down but eventually earned a partial scholarship to a small school on the east coast. This is not what Steve had anticipated and it became a source of contention between father and son. Steve withdrew his praise; Jim left football and played other sports. At this point, Steve focused his attention on the youngest sons, Andrew and Josh, hoping to create professional football players. The younger boys loved that they were now getting the attention, and knew how to keep the applause coming. They practiced two hours a day and scrimmaged against each other. They fought over who was the better player. Steve encouraged this battle, always cheering the victor and making loud comments that Josh was the better player. This set up a heated battle between the two.

I watched these boys at a high school alumni game where Josh lined up against his brother, Andrew. I have never heard more male trash talk in all my life. The sibling rivalry was quite apparent because their father's love and an A+ on their ego scorecard were at stake. That day, Andrew won his father's praise. Josh immediately went home to practice because he had to regain acceptance by his father. Josh became an outstanding player and the better he became, the more he was admired by his father, his schoolmates and even their parents. Every compliment garnered that A+ accompanied by a shot of positive neurochemical release. Unfortunately, as with most drugs, an addict needs more and more of the substance to get the same rush.

Josh is now obsessed with the game. Everything in his life revolves around whether or not he is the best player. Other teams fly him to different venues to be their hired gun. He has received his first contact from a professional NFL recruiter. Football became an obsession, feeding the insatiable ego. Unfortunately, the dark side of this striving is that Josh cries into a towel when his team loses. These are a child's tears, a child who knows that he will not be loved if he loses. He must continue to win or his world will crumble. In reality, this response could be beneficial as it presents the opportunity to transcend his fears with self-acceptance and love. It is likely that life will continue to create circumstances where he can confront this obsession and learn to love himself for who he is without the need for an A+ on the ego scorecard.

The ego seeks classic battlegrounds for comparative supremacy. These battlegrounds are power, money, intelligence, physical strength, endurance, physical appearance, and materialism. The ego constantly searches for chinks in its own armor and avoids losing at all costs. On the other hand, the ego is very creative and also looks for new venues to feel superior. An example is the manipulation of archetypes. The ego thrives in relationships where one partner is considered the winner, whether that is between husband and wife, coworkers or amongst children. Usually, the alpha or stronger person in the relationship is in power, but sometimes the archetypal Victim or Martyr holds the power.

When people feel internal chaos, it is frightening and can lead to misery. These people embody the phrase "misery loves company." To feel better, they use the strategy of spreading their misery around. They mentally manipulate others drawing others into fear, hatred, or anger. These controllers feel empowered when they coerce others into actions that they would never do otherwise. They thrive in this power. The more disconnected these people are from their inner higher self, the more they inflict their chaos and pain onto others.

The struggle between our ego and our soul is remarkable. Our culture abounds with stories about this internal battle. Picture a young man filled with testosterone facing a decision. Immediately, a little devil pops up on one of his shoulders and screams loudly, "Take control of anything you want. It's there for you." In that same moment, the little white angel appears on the other shoulder whispering the wisdom that he feels in his heart, but prefers to forget. The devil's wants are succulent and exciting yet temporary. There is usually a huge downside to making that choice. Youth wants it all, and wants it now, period. The devil/ego plans and strategizes to discredit the angel/soul and the voice of wisdom. However, as this young man grows and matures, the angel's wisdom, the soul perspective, proves time and again to be the better choice. The devil brings chaos while the angel brings peace.

Each of the four personality colors has strategies to soothe the ego. The more we are aware of our ego strategies, the quicker we listen to the soul.

The Red personality typically goes for the classics of power, control, strength, and materialism such as fast cars, huge houses and lots of money.

Reds are admired in our society because they know how to attain these things that others want. They embody the positive archetypes of Provider and Warrior. Reds battle their way up the ladder of success employing victory as a prominent life motif. Reds use the negative Victim archetype when they are unable to thrive as Providers or Warriors. The Victim develops if their parents rewarded them for being hurt or losing a competition. Negative strategies are used when people realize they don't have the skills to compete, or when their expectations and fantasies about life oppose reality. This realization is the definition of stress. When people feel loved by their parents and have been positively reinforced, they will have enough internal self-esteem that they will choose the positive archetypes.

The Orange personality embodies the Caretaker archetype and finds strength through a large group of supportive friends. Their network of friends returns the care taking with loyal support. When something goes wrong or they are depressed, Oranges easily find friends to sympathize and support the situation. The positive Caretaker is very charismatic and fun to be around and are extremely considerate, and thoughtful. When others are not as considerate, thoughtful or giving, the Orange ego wins by being the better person. Oranges turn to the negative Martyr archetype when they are hurt by others. This archetype is a natural strategy because Orange's life goal is to win approval from others. When Oranges lack a sense of inner wholeness, they frequently become naysayers who find fault with anything that requires action. When the Naysayer archetype is active, unmotivated Oranges stay in their caves, refusing to challenge life. They find people to take care of them while they remain hidden from painful criticism. They withdraw in moodiness, excessive alone time or even medication.

Yellow personalities are great providers and problem solvers. Since their mind typically works faster than the other personalities with the same IQ, they seek praise for doing what they do well. Yellows are efficient, disciplined and inventive. They discern the technical rundown between two gadgets and appreciate mechanical knowledge. Yellows do not pay lip service to their own beliefs, they live them wholeheartedly. They are hardwired for judgment due to their refined moral compass. While the strategy of raising the bar high enough to be beyond intellectual reproach can be a positive archetype, this rigidity is indicative of low self-esteem.

This also makes Yellows capable of self-praise to get scorecard plusses. One Yellow friend is proud of his analytical ability to determine the right answer; yet he also analyzes himself saying, "I also have the ability to overanalyze things just a little too far to the point of overthinking and then I am paralyzed." The Servant, the Cynic, and the Skeptic are the negative archetypes. It is important that Yellows understand that negativity quickly spirals into inner and outer judgment. Extremely negative Yellows delight in manipulating others.

Positive Green archetypes are the Lover, the Healer and the Peacekeeper. Greens are capable of receiving and giving unconditional love. They are creative, expansive thinkers, and are not tied to the process of moving from A to Z. This allows greens to brainstorm and make jumps that few others are capable of. Great at leading with a kind heart and encouragement, Greens look for connection with the world and have many deep friendships. Greens give friends praise for their activism and the causes they support. Greens are needy when they don't get love. The negative archetypes include the Egotist and Narcissist which strategize with hopelessness, self- pity and the endless search for praise. The purpose of these negative strategies is manipulation for external power and self-esteem.

All of us contain and use all of the archetypes depending on the situation. We choose our strategy based on our matrix but the common denominator is the ego steers us towards situations where we excel, and guides us away from potential conflict. This is done by using positive and negative archetypes to expand the ego's influence and gain the upper hand. The ego usually avoids grief, sadness, betrayal, abandonment, despair, anger, resentment or yearning. Egos need to be right and prefer to be around like-minded people. The ego's definition of unity is *everyone having the same beliefs*. However, this is just the ego grasping once again.

The more we dwell in the soul perspective, the more tolerant and accepting we become. It is inescapable to want to be right but the level of discomfort we display and the actions that we take indicate just how much the ego rules our thoughts. If our blood boils when we hear someone spouting off a belief system that is different from our own, the little red guy on our shoulder is screaming in our ears. Human history is filled with the horrors of war based on wanting our race, religion or ideology to win. Most human tragedy comes from our desire to put a check in the A+ column on the ego scorecard.

Gratefully, our soul perspective embodies a completely different set of beliefs and guidelines. This perspective seeks neither plusses nor conformity and personifies acceptance, gratitude, tolerance, oneness, openness, awe, and joy. The soul perspective is process oriented rather than goal oriented. There is not scorecard for the soul.

Let's imagine two young men going to the weight room to work out. Being ego-based, the young men are motivated by each others' opinions and the need to be stronger. We'll call one of the young men Ego-Man. He walks into the gym and immediately compares himself with the other men. He gauges their size and the amounts they lift. As he lifts weights, he imagines how big he'll get and how others will admire him when they see his size. He checks the mirror for progress and a quick snapshot of how buff he looks. He's just finished checking off the plus column when the door pops open and in swaggers a bigger, stronger and handsomer competitor. Seen through the eyes of the ego, his self-perspective shatters because he is now less than the other guy. Ego-man's esteem is losing and he energetically shrinks. He becomes depressed. It's tough to say if he will lift even harder, or give up lifting altogether because the ego avoids less-than situations. The soulful choice is self-acceptance.

The Soul-based man is also working out. As he lifts, a different set of thoughts are going through his mind. He relishes being alive. He builds up his muscles because he delights in strengthening his body, mind, and soul. He appreciates and cares for his body as a temple and looking in the mirror reminds him of his amazing experiences. Just then a larger toned and good-looking man begins to exercise with the weights right next to him. Soul-man acknowledges him without playing the comparison game. Both men get their exercise, each with a different perspective and different results. Yet both men were at the same gym at the same time using comparable machines. One lived in fear, pumping heart-stopping adrenaline, and the other lived in the glow of the peace-producing neurochemicals that circulated through his system.

Judgment is clearly at play in the Ego-man example. Judgment is usually accompanied by shame, blame, guilt, embarrassment, hierarchy, righteousness, pomposity, condescension, and so on. There is a motivating sense of power and adrenaline when we are judgmental and righteous. The more self-righteous we become, the more power we wield. This is very exciting to the ego. This empowers the ego-judge to speak with even greater authority and zeal. As I mentioned earlier, Orange and Yellow ego-based personalities have a knack for self-judgment. These personalities need to become aware of how much they use this language. This reflects some very destructive internal beliefs. Then there are those who have lost themselves and just want to belong, to do the right thing, and to be accepted. There are also those whose mainframe program is based on shame, blame and guilt. These individuals will be susceptible to following the judge. As the judge's power grows with the insatiable needs of the ego, they move to the next level. This is the level of fundamentalism. This is the world of absolutes, literalism and uniformity of dogmas.

The ego scorecard is very limiting as the fear of not being good enough blocks so much potential. Imagine that you are four-years-old, in pre-school and just painted a picture. The teacher passes by your desk and stops by a child right next to you and praises his picture. She tells him that he has a real talent as an artist. The teacher then looks at your painting, but has no reaction. The ego scorecard gets a minus sign and you never try painting again. But what if the teacher's response was because she only likes pictures that stay within the lines, or pictures that are exact duplications? Maybe your picture is impressionistic and emotional. Maybe the teacher abandoned her own artistic dreams. That one slight may have destroyed a young Picasso or O'Keeffe. It is unfortunate that we quickly buy into the contrived and fictitious beliefs of others around us. Living and dying by the scorecard means losing the chance to truly discover ourselves. Guidance doesn't come from others; it comes from the soft, soothing voice of the soul. Guidance gives us the freedom to experience the *now* and to become exactly who we are meant to be. Soul allows us the free will to expand and unfold. The soul perspective doesn't compete because the internal comparison of good enough is not an issue. The soul revels in the bliss of receiving.

Today is the day for us to practice a new perspective. The next time we walk into a situation and our ego begins the comparison game, let's take away its scorecard and rip it up. We *can* refuse to listen to other's opinions. Let's commit to the freedom to be our radically unique selves without dreading others' scorecards. There is simply no reason why we cannot be anything we wish. It doesn't matter if we want to be an artist, an athlete, a physicist, or a musician. Anything is possible as long as we feed the path with unbounded joy. When we *do* become artists or musicians, joy ensures that our work will not mimic anyone else's. Whatever path we choose, we can discover and claim our talents. This is how we release the ego scorecard and hold fast to who we are.

Chapter 14

THE PATH TO INNER PEACE

I remember seeing a poster about inner peace years ago. It contained a fairly long list of experiences describing living a life of inner peace. The experiences and insights were all different but I remember two specific items on the list: the ability to enjoy living in a mansion, and the ability to enjoy living in a shack. At the time, I didn't believe that one could achieve inner peace by living in a shack but the poster opened my mind. I learned that embodying inner peace means being able to enjoy every moment without placing value judgments on experiences. Those with inner peace do not judge experiences good or bad, positive or negative; they just take them in.

A person must understand and see themselves clearly and intimately to achieve this state. We must be able to self-diagnose, not beating ourselves down or puffing ourselves up. To be a good self-diagnostician, we must reach deep into our inner matrix and be able to extract meaning for our actions. Another aspect of knowing ourselves intimately is to have a self-intimacy internal dialogue that allows us to listen to and rely upon our inner wisdom. This develops by spending time alone in quiet. A good example is people who in pursuing personal growth and change, take vows of silence so that they can hear their inner voice. The easiest way for me to do this is by taking a long walk, if not days of walking, alone in a beautiful forest.

Acceptance is an important part of this state of being. I understand acceptance as two branches off the same tree. On one branch, we are able to accept everything just as it is. There is no need to change anything because we are open to receiving life without wishing things to be other than they are. When we accept what is, there is no need to fear anything. We don't fear what other people think, what people will say, or if we will have enough food, money or material objects. We will also not fear people liking or loving us based on having or not having these possessions. We don't fear shortfalls because we no longer *interpret* experiences as scarcity. Because we experience life for what is, instead of what it is not, we are open to abundance. People who live with acceptance are capable of manifesting great change in their lives. There is a mantra often adopted by people working on living with acceptance, "It is what it is." If we hear these words or we begin to say them ourselves, we are on the path toward inner peace.

Accepting the world as it is includes accepting others as they are. I have talked a lot about people who strive to make themselves feel better by judging others. This strategy must work for them as they continue to pursue this tactic and refine it to a very sophisticated level. Judging others as good or bad, right or wrong, better or worse, moral or immoral, or any other dualistic term, indicates that person has yet to live a life with acceptance and consequently inner peace. The goal is to live a life free of comparisons. A life with inner peace is not driven by the ego's scorecard and does not participate in the poisons of the Buddhist philosophy. There is no need to grasp, push away or live in ignorance.

The other branch of acceptance is forgiveness. When we feel wronged by someone, we become very angry because we feel an injustice has been done to us. The perpetrator has acted against our core beliefs, theology, friends, or family and we feel wronged and hurt. There is a tendency toward revenge and to settle the score, an eye for an eye. But revenge does not take us down the path to inner peace. Forgiveness is a big step in that direction.

Anger does a great amount of damage, to our own self and to others, as it cycles in our thoughts. This process constantly releases negative neurochemicals which cause us physical strain and sucks joy from our lives. Hate and anger against another creates an energetic link allowing negative emotions from others to affect us. When we release the hate, that link is broken, and the negativity no longer affects us. One of the greatest teachings of Christian philosophy is the call to love and forgive.

The final step in this process is not to use forgiveness as a means to feel righteous and superior. This comes from a false notion that we have the power to grant or deny acceptance of the other person. Acceptance implies that there is never judgment about good or bad; no one is the judge and no one is the victim. The incident is plainly accepted. We learn from and adapt to the experience, and the actions of others are completely accepted.

It's interesting to think about what life would be like without the tethers of fear and worry. Living with inner peace breeds excitement because there is no fear. We say, "Yes!" to life and participate in as many experiences as possible. There is a sense of wonder and joy; facial wrinkles brought on by frowning are transformed into laugh lines. This state of mind makes everything more beautiful. When we feel peaceful inside, we talk less and say more. Our speech becomes a vehicle to the things we love or that touch us deeply. We can say less if the ego is not trying to influence every outcome of daily events.

Mystical texts from different disciplines highlight enlightenment as key to finding inner peace. One characteristic of enlightenment is the knowing of Oneness, the connection to the Divine Source of All. The Torah teaches that when Moses came down from Mount Sinai, having talked to or merged with God, he brought back one of the oldest prayers of the Jewish faith. It reads, "Sh'ma Yisrael. Adonai Eloheinu. Adonai Ehad. Hear O Israel. God is our God. God is One." Hebrew is a deep language with multiple interpretations and the last two words of this prayer, "Adonai Ehad," can be translated in different ways. The word "Ehad" can mean one, alone or oneness; therefore, this phrase could mean that there is just one God, or that God is Oneness. The idea that God is Oneness is the great mystery, beyond the capacity of most people to contemplate. The Oneness of God indicates that everything is God; everything is the Creator in the process of creating. It means that we are a part of this creating. We are inside of Creation, creating, intimately a part of God. This also means that everything that exists, seen or unseen, is a part of this special oneness. This is a very powerful statement, which seems to be self-evident to those who live in inner peace. Once we take away this separation, we can realize the Oneness of all with even greater depth

I have never met anyone who exhibits all of these characteristics of inner peace at the same time. But I have met people who experience these qualities at different times in their lives for different lengths of time. The more they do inner work, the more consistent their experience of living with inner peace becomes.

Chapter 15

COMMITTING TO THE PROCESS: A CASE STUDY

IT WAS A BIG DAY, a day of remembering what the soul journey is all about. One of my patients, whom I will call Dr. Yellow-Green, came in very upset because the cancer treatments weren't working. Two years prior, she was diagnosed as having Stage Four breast cancer. She had tried many therapies, some that had slowed the various tumor growths, but none that had eliminated the tumors. The cancer had metastasized to the bones, brain and liver. She underwent the most aggressive chemotherapy, which caused her to lose her hair and feel terrible and tired. Since being diagnosed, she had gone about her life without letting the fatal news drag her down, yet this indicated avoidance rather than acceptance.

We opened the day discussing her feelings. She expressed grief, disappointment, frustration, anger and betrayal. Despite the invasive chemotherapy, the tumor markers were staying high. Her expectations about her healing process were shattered and she was dismayed that her life savings was depleted to no avail. She was at the end of her rope. Yet, Dr. Yellow-Green repeated how much she had changed. She insisted that if she healed, cancer would never come back again. She claimed that if she had this one chance, she would use her story to help others in the same situation. She pleaded and negotiated with God, "It's not fair. It's not fair, why me?" However, this unsigned contract would only lead to more disappointment or even betrayal because such contracts and expectations never go exactly the way we wish.

All of this talk told me that my client and I needed to discuss the inherent gifts in facing imminent mortality. This knowledge can be the wake-up call that motivates us to squeeze the last drops of life's nectar. Death reminds us how much energy and time is spent on resentment, anger, and the need to be right. Succulent days filled with infinite potential and love become lost in negativity. Wake-up calls return the soul's message that our lives can be filled with joy and awe or with negativity and fear. It is our choice. This message is undeniable to terminally ill patients who live with the daily reminder that death is near, and no one knows what happens after death. This uncertainty is a scary place. Yet this uncertainty keeps them on the path of learning *how to live.* These patients find ways to expand every aspect of life and to let go of what doesn't matter. They no longer sweat the little stuff. Living becomes all important.

I asked Dr. Yellow-Green, "How can you return to living life where the vast majority of your feelings are beneficial? How can you commit to the process of wiping out belief systems that create negative emotions and behaviors? I explained this meant choosing beneficial, harmonious thoughts with circulating, feel-good neurochemistry. Dr. Yellow-Green's thoughts, beliefs and feelings were her choice. She had been choosing the beliefs that led to resentment, betrayal and other sour-tasting emotions but she could allow life to feel sweeter. This is not to say that we should never experience negative emotions. The process is to *experience, feel, adapt,* and *function.* To reach this point we must let go of negative beliefs that lock us into an endless loop of life-stealing sourness. We must understand the childhood source of our motivations and feelings. Finally, we need to become aware of negative archetypes and feelings such as shame, blame and arrogance, as well the other symptoms listed in the CV & GV category. Ultimately, life is very short. How will we commit to the process of getting rid of our issues? How will we commit to the beliefs that bring us happiness and joy? Can we stay motivated without the need for cancer to remind us that we are missing out on life?

I was in my early 20s the first time I received a preliminary diagnosis of cancer, the same type of cancer my father had died of. This scare caused me to completely change. My outlook transformed and I appreciated life in a way I had never dreamed possible. I saw joy and miracles all around me. I want all of us to live this way. Appreciation could end the negative fears and beliefs that lead to war and suffering. Appreciation changes everything and *it is possible.*

Dr. Yellow-Green initially resisted when I invited her to accept that she might die from cancer. She resisted because she believed this thinking would allow the cancer to kill her. I explained that this would actually release the daily, subconscious fear. Dying of cancer was her dominant thought. The rules of manifesting state that our overriding thoughts, whether conscious or not, come true. At the same time, we cannot think ourselves to death when our soul chooses life. Our soul has more influence than our mind. Ultimately, Dr. Yellow-Green might not control whether she lives or dies from this cancer. However, she felt that cancer was a punishment and she was to blame. She asked, "Why me?" and vowed to live better, using what she learned if she was spared. However, her underlying beliefs ultimately produced a victim the more the cancer progressed. Dr. Yellow-Green's thoughts did not allow for joyful and life-healing neurochemistry. However, showing up, telling the truth, and doing her best while being unattached to the outcome is therapeutic. One can replace chaos with inner peace through experience and feeling. After discussing the downsides to avoidance and denial, Dr. Yellow-Green chose the path of acceptance. This gave her more energy to focus on wellness.

A chakra scan revealed Dr. Yellow-Green's issues of condescension and judgment towards herself and others. She emotionally admitted that this involved nearly every action and belief. This was her greatest addiction. Judgment made her feel superior, but at the same time, she judged every one of her own actions. This left her with feelings of not being good enough which made it difficult to overcome hardships. We focused on this belief system and found a new tactic to work deeper with this issue. For the first time, she committed in a profound way.

Her next issue was feeling cut off from the Divine. This issue presented in the 6th chakra which is different than if it had presented in the lower four. These chakras have more to do with human existence; 5th or 6th chakras issues are calls from the soul. Muscle testing confirmed that she needed to commit to bringing the soul's perceptions and existence to the forefront of her experience. Dr. Yellow-Green realized that she had not been practicing Qi Gong even though she wanted to and felt much better when she did. She had slowly gotten out of the habit. I felt her re-commit to life as she spoke. She described the many ways that she could engage her soul throughout each day. She was on fire.

Again, soul connection dots throughout the day create a solid line. Whether through meditation, Qi Gong, or by taking a slow, silent walk in nature, the soul will stay connected. This is the place of acceptance and knowing that everything is okay and will work out. I thanked Dr. Yellow-Green for returning me to my soul's perspective. Dr. Yellow-Green asked for an exercise or a technique that would help her reconnect to the right brain. I recited:

Nothing is good or bad. There is no past and there is no future. I *choose* to receive the most from each experience in my life.

I have talked about the principle of doing 1000 things right and only one thing wrong, but we spend most of our time concentrating on the one thing wrong. That one issue fills your conscious thoughts. You can cycle it over and over to where it fills all of your attention units throughout the day and even your sleep. By now, you know that it is a choice how we perceive our life. No one can make you feel badly. Only you can choose a belief that can turn a great life into a horrible one where everything is going wrong. I would like to share a wonderful practice that can help you choose to change this negative programming.

A friend of mine turned me on to the work of Harvard professor, Shawn Achor. He is the author of the bestselling book, *The Happiness Advantage*. Shawn has become the world's leading expert on the connection between happiness and success and his TED talk, which was my introduction to him, has been viewed by over 2 million people.

Professor Achor hypothesized that if people brought to mind something they were grateful for three times a day their outlook on life would improve and they would have positive health implications. The researchers would measure results subjectively by asking the participants if they felt happier and more positive. They would also look at objective measures such as blood pressure, pulse rates and blood chemistry changes. The results were clear. The test subjects reported a greater sense of well-being and the objective measures were improved. All this changed with a minimum of effort.

Shawn Achor and his team also believed that having a positive view on life is really more the natural state of the being. We have a great feedback mechanism to see the world through a positive lens versus the negative one most of us see through. We seem to be brainwashed into prioritizing the negatives in life with society encouraging belief in negative outcomes. We are trained through the news on TV, magazines, tabloids, and gossip. Somehow most of us resonate with a negative view on life that creates negative implications in our body.

I thought deeply about this research. If bringing to mind things we are grateful for three times a day created such positive results, what would happen if we did this more often? If a little bit is good, wouldn't more be better? So I decided to do my own research. I set my watch alarm to go off every day at 9:30 AM and which time I would think about something that I was grateful for, something I had really enjoyed or that was going wonderfully. I would repeat this process every hour thereafter until bed time. All day I heard the hourly beeps from my watch which reminded me to awaken to the positive real-life that I had fallen asleep to. The reality was that life was filled with amazing moments that I was letting go by unacknowledged. I begin the practice again every morning and throughout each day.

This practice creates moments or dots during the day that ground you to what I think is a more true reality. Each of these dots represents times where you are slowing down, calming the neurological system and perhaps altering your brain wave state that can make you more aware of the wisdom within you. These are soul moments where we break through the tricks of the ego and the illusion of the five physical senses. The more dots you create through your day the more you will shift your entire experience of life. If you add more and more dots to your day soon the experience will be that of a solid line. These moments that you are creating, tend to spread themselves out in front of and behind the focal moment. There is carryover between the dots and the dots turn into a line or a experience.

The first three days of my experiment were quite novel and enjoyable. I was a little surprised by how many good things there were in a day that I had forgotten about. But then I experienced a resistance to change. Though this practice was fun for the first three days, it began to seem like an extra task that distracted me from other things I felt I had to do. This whole practice didn't seem productive enough for me to continue.

I thought at that moment how we as a society need these firecracker moments to keep our interest. I told myself that resistance to change is expected and once realizing that it was time now to put the resistance to the side and move forward with these subtle elegant moments. I had to realize that these little moments might be doing something bigger than I realized in my moments of impatience and need to get the things on my lists done. I instantly thought of two principles. The first one was that the greatest power comes from the most elemental things. The second was that, the thing that I thought might be harming me the most might just be saving my life. These principles must be expanded metaphorically to understand their potential. I pushed through the inertia of change and my work went deeper.

The more I stayed with this practice the more my perspective changed every day. My experiences were amplified. It reminded of how my mother looked at art and was mesmerized and moved emotionally by its form. I would see others walk by the same painting, seemingly missing the whole message. It reminded me of how my son would eat food as a little child. As he would chew, he would be quietly chanting Yum Yum Yum Yum Yum Yum Yum. We fondly referred to this as making 'yummy noises." Try it sometime. Your food will taste better because you're drawing your focus into the act of eating and tasting.

I also noticed that I cherished experiences beyond the moment they occurred. Because I had focused on gratitude and happiness, experiences were embedded in my thoughts even more. This allowed them to spread out into other moments. I also found myself looking for the things that I would acknowledge the next time the beeper went off. I realized that I was looking for the positive and enjoyable things that were happening all around me. I was no longer taking them for granted. As I walked out of a supermarket, a cool breeze blew across my face and I stopped to feel it and revel in it. This triggered the different brain wave state or filter through which I was seeing my world. I instantly noticed how beautiful the blue sky looked spotted by clouds that seemed to be painted with so many shades of white. The wind that was moving around me was now also moving the leaves on the nearby tree so softly. All this was happening while I was pushing a shopping cart to my car in an asphalt parking lot lined by trees. I would not have had that experience if I had not pushed through the inertia of change. As I drove home, that moment began to shrink but it did not disappear. I still had the experience and I knew in less than an hour I would hear the beep beep beep of my alarm that would help me awaken once again to all the wonders of life I had previously been shutting out.

We must consciously make dots through the day because we will never be able to live in ecstasy all the time. There are times we must function differently to accomplish certain tasks but this practice is a great way to awaken and return to this positive state of gratitude and happiness. There are many roads that will lead to the same place. We must all find a way to awaken to life's beautiful gifts and hopefully along the way, we find a way to pierce the veil that separates our conscious mind from the consciousness of our soul. I hope you will integrate the practice of self-exploration in E3 to help you in your life.

Acknowledgement

I AM THANKFUL TO THE chiropractic world that gave us Dr. George Goodheart and Applied Kinesiology. These healing arts allowed me the elbow room to think and expand my practice outside of the box. I acknowledge Dr. Scott Walker for doing the ground breaking work of using muscle testing to help us see the emotional-mind-body connection.

I thank Dr. Carol Ritberger for introducing me to the connection between auras and behavior. I would like to express great thanks to my favorite clinical psychology instructor, Dr. George Mulder of Chapman College. I enjoyed every one of your classes and am thankful that you encouraged, even pushed, me to explore and develop new techniques that had not yet been used in psychology. You recognized and nurtured something inside of me that was needed in the healing arts world. I thank all of you for helping me to recognize and discover my life's work.

I cannot thank my mother enough for her gift of many years of self-healing through therapy. She refused to let me inherit all the dysfunction that was an integral part of her family. Most of humanity runs from the reality that we are emotional beings; yet an optimal life revolves around how well we process our emotions and fears. Life is happier and longer when we make experiencing and processing our emotions a daily routine. I remember my mother actively involving and teaching me how to process my emotions. Though we sometimes yelled or cried, she taught me that it was okay to express my anger, as long as it was constructive. Once we got everything off of our chests, we asked, "Okay, how do we work this out from here?" Working out issues was like taking a shower or brushing my teeth. It needed to be done on a regular basis. I cannot express enough gratitude that Margaret Mehring was my mother.

I would also like to thank my beautiful family for supporting me through this process.

Resources

Rabbi David Cooper
God is a Verb: Kabbalah & the Practice of Mystical Judaism
Riverhead Books. New York, NY. 1997

Daniel J. Benor, M.D.
Spiritual Healing: Scientific Validation of A Healing Revolution
Vision Publications. Southfield, MI. 2001

Dr. Brian L. Weiss, M.D.
Many Lives, Many Masters
Simon & Schuster, New York, NY. 1988

Michael Newton, PH.D.
Destiny of Souls: New Case Studies of Life Between Lives
Llewellyn Publications. St. Paul, MN. 2000

Robert Ornstein and Richard F. Thompson
The Amazing Brain
Houghton Mifflin Company. Boston, MA. 1984.

Jill Bolte Taylor, PH.D.
My Stroke of Insight: A Brain Scientist's Personal Journey
Penguin Group. New York, NY. 2006
Jill Bolte Taylor, PH.D. Jill Bolte-Taylor's Stroke of Insight. March 2008.
<http://www.ted.com/talks/jill_bolte_taylor_s_powerful_stroke_of_insight.html>

Ken Cohen
<http://www.qigonghealing.com>

Hong Liu
<http://www.qimaster.com>

Yun Xiang Tseng
<http://www.wudangtao.com>

Shawn Achor
http://goodthinkinc.com/media/

Biography

DR. WILLIAM D. MEHRING, a chiropractor, has combined his knowledge of applied kinesiology, psychology, hypnotherapy and the energetic healing practice of Qi Gong, into a restorative process called E3: Emotional Energetic Evolution. Dr. Mehring transformed his personal healing crisis, which he calls his cosmic 2 x 4, into a commitment for self-healing. His pledge to listen to his inner voice, as well as his body, transformed his life of physical and psychic pain, into alignment with his soul's purpose. Emotional Energetic Evolution is the alchemy that changes chaos into peace. Dr. Mehring's hope is for individuals and healing professionals to use this manual to treat and even bypass illness, trauma and tension.

Dr. Mehring lives in California's San Luis Obispo County, where he is currently writing his next book about personality types and their relationships. He enjoys a SLO life filled with family, friends, hiking, surfing, and volleyball. He lectures locally as well as internationally.

For more information, contact *www.findingpeaceinchaos.com*